Hands On Dyeing

Hands On Dyeing

Betsy Blumenthal & Kathryn Kreider

Illustrations by Ann Sabin

Acknowledgments

Our special thanks to Joan Sterrenberg and Budd Stalnaker, professors in the Textile Department of the School of Fine Arts at Indiana University, who introduced us to controlled dyeing, and to all the graduates of their program who have contributed to the dissemination of dyeing techniques throughout the country with their teaching and their artwork, and to all our students, who have shared their enthusiasm with us in workshops over the past several years and who have taught us how to teach dyeing.

We also wish to thank the following individuals for their essential assistance: Gregory Blumenthal and Pat Penner for demystifying the computers; Nancy Brouillard for her help with Dyekit, and Dana Blumenthal for tie-dye experimentation; Claire Kiehle and Anne Wulf for their dyeing, weaving, spinning, knitting and crocheting, and their support throughout.

Photography by Joe Coca
Typesetting by Marc M. Owens
Photo of authors by Sidney Sanders

 Interweave Press
201 East Fourth Street
Loveland, Colorado 80537

Library of Congress Catalog Number 88-12260
ISBN 0-934026-36-X
First printing: 10M:588:HP:CL
Second printing: 10M:589:HP
Third printing: 10M:493:HP

 Library of Congress Cataloging-in-Publication Data

Blumenthal, Betsy
  Hands on dyeing / Betsy Blumenthal & Kathryn Kreider :
illustrations by Ann Sabin.
    p. cm.
  ISBN 0-934026-36-X : $8.95
  1. Dyes and dyeing—Textile fibers. I. Kreider, Kathryn. 1950-
  II. Title.
TT853.B58 1988
7461'3--dc 19

CONTENTS

To buy this many colors of the same yarn would be very expensive, but to dye them is low-cost and easy.

1

Introduction

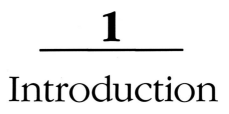

Dyeing is a miraculous technique. In a matter of moments a yarn or fabric changes from one color to another, and even experienced dyers feel a sense of magic and excitement with each dye run. There is always great pleasure in seeing freshly dyed yarns and fabrics ready for the next project.

Dyeing has often been entwined in mathematical complexity or shrouded in oversimplification. On the one hand, many people who teach dyeing have established systems for the home dyer which attempt to duplicate industry's standards. On the other hand, suppliers of grocery-store dyestuffs have simplified the technology so much that the dyer cannot reasonably predict the color which will result or its permanence.

We would like to strike a balance between these extremes. We have been dyeing for nearly fifteen years, and have found that a certain amount of organization is necessary for good results. We have also found that we can obtain excellent results with a simplified measuring system and by using readily available household equipment.

The key to success in dyeing is consistency. It is important to establish a dye procedure—which includes a dye recipe and a measuring system—and to stick with it.

This book is written for the weaver, quiltmaker, or other fiber artisan who wants the benefits of systematic dyeing but does not have the equipment, time, or inclination to do laboratory-style dyeing. The information is designed to give controlled, repeatable, predictable results with a minimum of complexity. We recognize that there are many different sources for information on dyeing and that some of these may conflict with the information we present. We have synthesized information from many sources to arrive at our instructions for each of the kinds of dye that we have included. Ours is not to be considered the final word, but hopefully the first word for home dyers. Our goal is to make dyeing accessible to everyone who wants to employ this simple process for useful and beautiful results.

The textile craftsperson seeking a personal palette of colors will find the advantages of home dyeing to be compelling. In the first place, suppliers of fiber, yarn, and fabric must limit the range of colors that they make available. Often a necessary color can be bought only in the wrong yarn size or fiber type. Without the ability to dye yarn, the craftsperson is left with a limited choice of colors, in the types of yarns and put-ups dictated by current fashion. The home dyer, on the other hand, can hold large quantities of white yarns or fabrics in inventory, and then quickly and easily produce the colors needed. Even allowing for the occasional unsuitable color which may result, the cost of purchasing neutral yarns or fabrics plus dyes is

Pillars *by Betsy Blumenthal*

much less than the cost of stocking a variety of fibers in a wide range of colors. Furthermore, the home dyer can create shades unavailable at any price, such as subtle gradations of closely related shades, or skeins with specific multicolor dye effects. In addition, leftover materials can be effectively utilized through overdyeing, existing colors can be harmonized, bright colors can be muted, or undesirable colors can be altered.

As with any craft, it takes a little practice to develop the skills for successful home dyeing. The basic principles of controlled dyeing are:

1. Use measured amounts of water, dye, fiber, and chemical assistants in the dyebath.

2. Follow an established time schedule.

3. Keep track of the recipes used and the colors obtained.

The recipes for applying dyes to fiber are similar to cooking recipes, except that they are shorter and easier to follow.

Afterimage *by A. Nicholson*

You will discover a wide variety of synthetic dyes to choose from for home dyeing. The dye industry periodically develops a new dye or upgrades an old one, so the range of dyes is ever-increasing. Dye repackagers buy dyes in bulk, package them in reasonably priced, usable quantities, and distribute them for home use. Most of the dyestuffs for use on natural fibers can be easily obtained and are safe to use. In this book we will include dye recipes for several kinds of dyes: union dyes, fiber-reactive dyes, acid dyes, and pre-metallized dyes.*

Our system employs an easy way of measuring and mixing dyes to control color. With our system, we can create **color gradations** and **predictable, reproducible colors.** Color gradations can range from light to dark, from bright to dull, around the color wheel from one hue to another, or across the color wheel from a color to its complement. These effects are achieved by carefully varying the amount of dye, or combinations of dyes, in each dyebath. By repeating any recipe using the same fiber, it is possible to duplicate any color produced earlier. (Repeating the recipe on other fibers, or different amounts of fiber, will produce related hues.)

Special dye effects can be achieved by keeping dye away from some parts of the fiber. Familiar withholding or **resist techniques** are tie-dye, wrapped resist, and batik. Dyes can also be painted, sprayed, sponged, printed, or otherwise placed on the fiber. These techniques are called **direct application** or **surface design techniques.** Once the basics are mastered you'll have this wide variety of dye techniques at your command.

---

*We considered including disperse dyes, since these will dye synthetic fibers, but concluded that they are not practical for home use. In our trials with disperse dyes on polyester/cotton fabric the colors were pale and uninteresting, and the fumes from the carrier required for dyeing polyester were noxious.

2

Getting Started: Basic Dyeing Techniques

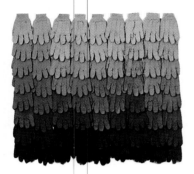

Handscape *by A. Nicholson*

Dyeing your own fibers is easy and fun. Dyeing is not expensive, time-consuming, or dangerous. In fact, following a dye recipe is like following the simplest cooking procedure and requires only a small investment in supplies and materials.

Most dyeing is **immersion dyeing.** In immersion dyeing the fiber is placed in a dyebath which contains water, dyes, and sometimes chemical assistants for a specified amount of time. An average dye run takes approximately one-and-one-half hours.

The best way to learn about dyeing is with an actual dye run. In Project 1 we provide you with two simple dye recipes: one for dyeing four shades of one color, and the other for dyeing four related colors. We have written the instructions for dyeing either cotton yarn or cotton fabric. We have also included instructions for making colorful table mats with the yarn or fabric which you create. The necessary dyes, equipment, and materials are available at local grocery, yarn, and fabric stores. Many items you already have at home. However, we recommend that you obtain a set of pots and measuring equipment which you can keep separate from your regular cooking utensils and pots, since it can be difficult to remove all traces of the dye. Yard sales and secondhand stores are good sources.

It is important to handle dyes and chemicals carefully. Some people are allergic to dye powders. Wear dishwashing gloves when

---

**PREPARING FABRIC
FOR THE DYEPOT**

Your fabric must be washed to remove the sizing, unless the fabric has been purchased from a supplier that sells it prewashed and ready for dyeing. Fabric should be machine-washed with a mild detergent that does not contain whiteners and brighteners. Washing will also preshrink the fabric, if you use hot water. Since the fabric needs to be fully wet, leave it in the last rinse water or in a tub of plain water for about thirty minutes before you begin dyeing.

handling dyes. Cover your working surfaces with newspapers, to avoid staining your countertops. (If you do spill dye on your countertops it can be removed with an abrasive or liquid all-purpose cleanser.) Wear old clothes.

Read through the instructions for Project 1 and assemble all of your materials before you begin. Leave ample time to complete the dye run. Although the run should take approximately ninety minutes, you will probably need more time if this is your first experience with dyeing.

PREPARING YARN FOR THE DYEPOT

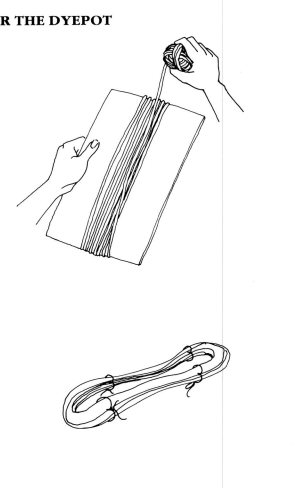

Step 1: Skeining the yarn. If the yarn to be dyed is not packaged in fold-type skeins (for example, the yarn we use for Project 1, Lily's Sugar 'n Cream Cotton, comes in pull skeins), then it must be wound into loose skeins so the dye can reach all of the fiber. If you do not have a skein winder, wind the yarn around a piece of cardboard. Fasten the ends of the skein together with a knot, and then tie each skein loosely with extra ties at three or four places around the skein. (It is handy to use a synthetic yarn which will not take the dye for these ties, because they will be easy to find and remove when the skein is ready to use. Another option is to use yarns from other man-ufacturers as ties, so they can be used as samples for your records of how different yarns react with the dyes.) If the yarn is already in fold-type skeins, make sure there are three or four loose ties around the skein.

Step 2: Washing the yarn. It is efficient, when possible, to wash your yarn just before you plan to dye it, so that the washing will also wet-out the fiber for dyeing. Use warm water and a small amount of liquid detergent. Gently wash and thoroughly rinse the fiber. Leave the fiber in the last rinse water for about thirty minutes to ensure that it is fully wet before you begin dyeing.

Project 1: Four-Color Placemats

designed, dyed, and constructed by Kathryn Kreider and Claire Kiehle

We recommend that you experience how easy it is to dye your own colors of yarn or fabric by trying this project before you read much farther. We've designed the project so that you can choose whether to work with yarns or fabric. This dye run features a shortcut method for measuring dye which is elegant in its simplicity. We call it the "easy dilution" method. There are two dye runs included, one which creates four shades of one color, and one which creates four different colors.

Equipment you will need:
- four plastic dye buckets, to hold at least 2 gallons each
- two 1-cup measures
- plastic measuring spoons
- dishwashing gloves
- cardboard to wind skeins (18" long × 6" wide) if you are dyeing yarn

Materials you will need:
For crochet mats: 16 to 20 ounces of white or unbleached cotton yarn (knitting-worsted size with approximately 50 yards per ounce) wound into skeins of 2 to 2½ ounces each. It is important that each of your skeins weighs the same amount as the others, but it does not matter if that amount is 2 or 2½ ounces. The yarn we used came in 2½-ounce skeins. We put one skein in each dyepot. Since you will need four skeins for each run, the eight skeins will be enough for both dye runs.

For quilted mats: Eight yards medium-weight natural-color 100% cotton fabric, cut into one-yard lengths. You will need four yards for each dye run.

Dyes you will need:
For the first four-color dye run you will need one package of any union dye (Rit, Cushing, etc.). Buy liquid dye if possible.

For the second four-color dye run you will need two colors of union dye. You will have enough dye left from your first dye run for one of your colors in the second run. We used Rit liquid dye in blue and yellow for the crochet mats, and blue and scarlet for the quilted mats.

Preparing your fibers:
See the insert box in this chapter for how to prepare your yarns or fabrics for dyeing. Leave the fibers to wet out while you prepare your dyebaths for the first dye run.

First-run dyebaths:
one-color dyeing with the easy-dilution method
1. If the dye you have is in liquid form, shake well, and pour ¼ cup of

Gather your equipment for the "easy dilution" dye method.

Add a little water to the dry dye powder to make a paste, then stir in the rest of the measured water.

the first color into one of the measuring cups. Reserve the rest to use in the second dye run. If your dye is in powdered form, you must first mix it into a liquid, as follows:

Place the entire package of dye in a measuring cup, add 1 tbsp hot water, and mix until the dye is thoroughly wet. Add warm water to this dye paste, gradually stirring with each addition until your dye solution equals ½ cup. Pour ¼ cup of this into the second measuring cup and reserve the remainder for the second dye run.

2. Put 1 gallon of *hot* water into each of your four dyepots.

3. With all four dyepots arranged in front of you (use newspaper to protect your kitchen surfaces), measure your dye into the pots as follows:

First: Add ¼ cup water to the ¼ cup of dye in your measuring cup. This brings the total to ½ cup. Mix well. Then, pour ¼ cup of this first dilution into dyepot 1.

Second: Refill the dye cup with ¼ cup water to the ½-cup line, mix well and pour ¼ cup of this second dilution into dyepot 2.

Third: Again fill the dye cup with water to the ½-cup line, mix well, and pour ¼ cup of this third dilution into dyepot 3.

Fourth: Refill the dye cup a final time with water to the ½-cup line, mix well and pour ¼ cup of this fourth dilution into dyepot 4. This completes the measuring-out of your dye. Discard the ¼ cup of dilute dye which remains in your cup (see drawing below).

4. Squeeze the excess moisture out of four skeins of yarn or four pieces of fabric which have been wetting out. Add one skein of yarn, or one piece of fabric, to each dyepot. Stir well. Continue to dye your material, stirring at frequent intervals for 30 to 45 minutes.

5. Pour out each dyepot and rinse the yarn or fabric thoroughly. Finally, wash all the yarn or fabric, rinse well, and hang to dry.

You have completed your first "easy-dilution" dyebath. By diluting the dye with water repeatedly before adding it to each dyebath, you systematically decreased the amount of dye going into each dyebath. You have learned that the lightness or darkness of a color depends on the quantity of dye in the dyebath. Al-

though some dye instructions suggest that the darkness of color can be controlled by the length of time the material is left in the dyebath, you will find this makes only a slight difference. Furthermore, this method is not easy to control. The easy-dilution method will always give an even gradation of colors like those you have just created. **This dye dilution method can be used with any type of dye.**

Now you are ready to try a two-color version of the easy-dilution dye method.

Second-run dyebaths: two-color dyeing with the easy-dilution method

The equipment, materials, dyes, and preparation of your fibers will be the same as in the first dye run.

1. You will have ¼ cup (or more) of dye left in the color used in your first dye run. If your dye is in powdered form, mix your second color of dye into a liquid following the instructions in step 1 of the first dye run. With the dye in liquid form, stir well, and pour ¼ cup of the first color into one of the measuring cups

In the easy-dilution dye method, the dye solution is diluted with water to make successively lighter colors in each pot.

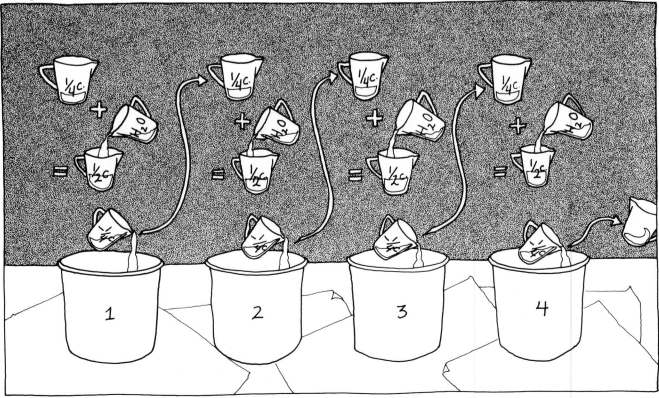

and ¼ cup of the second color into the other measuring cup.

2. Put 1 gallon of *hot* water into each of your four dyepots.

3. With all four dyepots arranged before you (use newspaper to protect your kitchen surfaces), measure first one color and then the other into the four pots as follows:

First: Start with color 1. Add water to the ¼ cup of dye to bring the total to ½ cup of dye, mix well, then pour ¼ cup of this first dilution into dyepot 1.

Second: Refill the dye cup with water to the ½-cup line, mix well and pour ¼ cup of this second dilution into dyepot 2.

Third: Again refill the dye cup with water to the ½-cup line, mix well, and pour ¼ cup of this third dilution into dyepot 3.

Fourth: Refill the dye cup with water to the ½-cup line, mix well, and pour ¼ cup of this fourth dilution into dyepot 4. This completes the measuring-out of your first dye color.

Now measure your second color in exactly the same way, proceeding from one dilution to the next, *except*

reverse the order in which you add the dye to the pots, as follows:

• Add ¼ cup of the first dilution to the fourth dyepot,
• add ¼ cup of the second dilution to the third dyepot,
• add ¼ cup of the third dilution to the second dyepot, and
• add ¼ cup of the fourth dilution to the first dyepot (see below).

Now both colors of dye have been added to each dyepot.

4. Squeeze the excess moisture out of the fabric pieces or yarn skeins, and add one piece of fabric or one skein of yarn to each pot. Stir well. Continue to dye material, stirring at frequent intervals for 30 to 45 minutes. Then thoroughly rinse the yarn or fabric from each pot, wash the yarns or fabric, and rinse again. Air dry.

MAKING THE TABLE MATS
Crocheted mats with striped pattern:
First dye-run colors: For our mats made from the four values of blue from dye run 1, we made two simple striped mats, each 13″ × 19″.

Use size H (or 8, or 5mm) crochet hook.

Gauge: 4½ sts per inch; 4 rows per inch.

Color Plan: Label your four blues in light to dark order, A, B, C, and D. Work 5″ color A, 5″ color B, 5″ color D, 5″ color C. Change the order of colors on each mat, as you wish.

Crochet instructions: Using color A, chain 50, turn. **Row 1:** skip 2 ch (counts as 1 sc), make 1 sc into each following ch to end, turn. **Row 2:** chain 1 (counts as 1 sc), skip first st of previous row, *make one sc into back loop only of next st, then one sc into front loop only of next st*, work across, ending with one sc. Turn. Repeat row 2 throughout.

Second dye-run colors: For our two mats from the two-color dye run, we used a more complicated stripe pattern that would have been too subtle if done in the close colors from dye run 1. The crochet stitch used was the same as that for the first four mats. Our first mat's color plan was as follows: 4″ color A, 1″ color D, 4″ color B, 1″ color D, 4″ color C, 1″ color D, ending with 4″ color B.

For a two-color mix in the easy-dilution method, one color is darkest in pot 1 while the other color is darkest in pot 4.

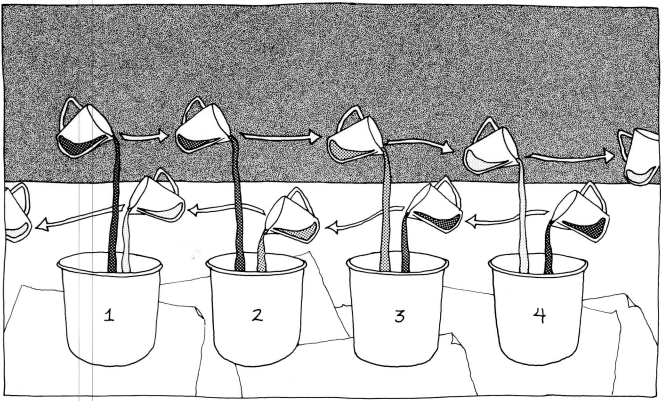

Project 1: Four-Color Placemats. *Use the easy-dilution method of dyeing several shades of one color or a gradation between two colors, and then crochet a set of placemats.*

Quilted mats with "triple rail fence" pattern:

For one placemat, finished size 18" × 12", cut: 3 pieces of fabric, 24" × 1", one from each of the three lightest shades; 1 piece 20" × 4", use background color of choice; and 1 piece 20" × 7", use same background color.

A note on fabric color choices: There is enough fabric to make four identical placemats from each of the two dye runs, or eight mats in all, if a different color is used for the background of each mat, or if an alternate fabric is used for the backing. We think that it is most interesting to vary the colors from mat to mat. For example, using fabric from the first dye run, we made two mats as described above with the three lightest shades in the rail-fence stripe and the darkest for the background. We made another two with the three darkest colors in the rail-fence stripe and the lightest for the background.

Quilting instructions:

1. Sew the three lightest-value strips together (pale next to light, light next to medium) with a 1/8" seam allowance. Press seams.

2. Cut this triple strip at lengths equal to the width of the strip to make nine squares. Assemble the squares, alternating vertical stripes with horizontal stripes. Rotate the horizontal squares so the darkest square appears first at the top, then at the bottom. (See illustration.)

3. Sew the squares together, using

To make the "triple rail fence" pattern, sew the long strips together so that they shade from lighter to darker. Then cut this assembled fabric into squares and rotate the pieces before sewing them together again.

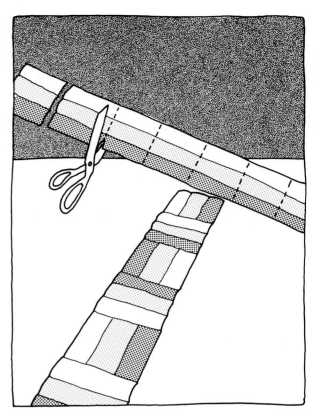

1/8" seams. Press each seam and carefully trim the long edges to straighten. Press the entire strip.

4. Sew one larger background piece along each long edge, using 1/8" seams. Press and trim edges to make the rectangles even.

5. Use a piece from the excess dyed fabric pieces, or another fabric, for the backing. Use a lightweight batting.

6. Assemble the top, batting, and bottom, and pin together. Machine quilt as follows: Sew along the seamline on each of the rail-fence pattern stripes. Then sew 1/4" away from that line, on each side. Working out from these lines, sew a line 1" away from the last sewn line. It is best to mark all the sewing lines before stitching. Bind the edges with a bias strip of dyed fabric or purchased bias tape.

Project 1: Four-Color Placemats. *The easy-dilution method used with cotton fabric will give you enough material for eight quilted placemats.*

3

Controlled Dyeing

We hope you have tried both of the dye runs in Project 1. If so, you are now the proud owner of eight new colors of yarn or fabric. In fact, you have already completed two controlled dye runs. **Controlled** or **systematic dyeing** is the method of producing exact colors by measuring both the material to be dyed and the dye (and chemical assistants, if required) for each dyebath. As you can see from Project 1, controlled dyeing is exactly like following a cooking recipe. Controlled dyeing allows for small changes in color, so you can create closely related colors or gradations from one color to another. Another important advantage of controlled dyeing is **reproducibility**, which means that the color recipes are measured accurately enough that you can re-create a particular color later.

Betsy dyed small amounts of ten colors to make her Heart Sweater. To buy ten colors would have been expensive, if possible at all, but dyeing them was quick and easy.

Rules of controlled dyeing

Any dyestuff can be used in a controlled or systematic way, since the rules of controlled dyeing hold true no matter what dyes are being used. Once you have mastered these basic rules the possibilities are limitless.

1. The **amount of fiber** to be dyed **must be measured,** by weight.
2. The **amount of dye** to be applied to the fiber **must be measured**. The amount of dye required depends on the weight of the fiber to be dyed and the darkness of the desired color.
3. **Any chemical assistants** to be added **must also be measured**, and the amounts depend on the weight of the fiber to be dyed.

Don't let this emphasis on measuring discourage you. As you saw in Project 1, a measuring system can be both powerful and simple. Although some dye instructions require precise and costly measuring equipment, our simplified system is inexpensive and effective. Our system depends on one basic fact: dyestuffs can be measured by *volume* (that is, by using teaspoons), instead of by *weight* (which requires an accurate metric scale).

Weighing the fiber

As mentioned above, you will need to weigh the materials to be dyed to obtain what is called the **weight of goods**. All other ingredients in a dye recipe are calculated with respect to this weight of goods (or **W.O.G.**). The more careful the measurements of your material, dye, and chemicals, the more accurate your results will be. It is useful, although not absolutely necessary, to have a scale in your dye workshop. Any scale that is relatively accurate will do.* Reasonably accurate measurements can also be obtained using the weight of the yarn on the label of the skein. Fabrics are not supplied with weights per yard. The average cotton quiltweight fabric weighs 100 grams per yard. The projects in this book will suggest different ways to simplify the measuring of your yarns and fabrics.

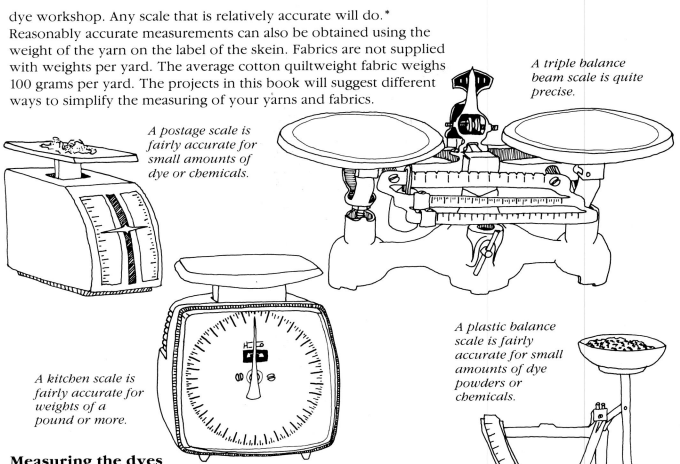

A triple balance beam scale is quite precise.

A postage scale is fairly accurate for small amounts of dye or chemicals.

A plastic balance scale is fairly accurate for small amounts of dye powders or chemicals.

A kitchen scale is fairly accurate for weights of a pound or more.

Measuring the dyes

Most dyes are available in powdered form, since they are easy to transport and they have the longest shelf life as powders. Powdered dyes are very concentrated; therefore, it is easiest to measure them accurately if they are diluted in water—that is, mixed into a **stock solution**.

There are two ways to measure powdered dyestuffs, either by weight or by volume. If you measure by **weight** you need a scale which is accurate to small amounts. If you measure dye by **volume** you need only small volume-measuring equipment, such as teaspoons, tablespoons, or small measuring cups. Although volume measurements are not as accurate as weight measurements, volume measuring is precise enough for most purposes, and it is much easier and more familiar for most of us.

There are actually only two disadvantages to measuring powdered dye by teaspoons, and neither turns out to be very important to the home dyer. First, it is not possible to be truly precise, because a teaspoon of dye measured at one time might not be exactly equivalent by weight to a teaspoon measured at another time. In practice, however, these differences are not large enough to significantly affect the final colors created. Second, when you measure by teaspoons, the precise concentrations of your stock solutions will

---

* You can get the most accurate measurements using a precise gram scale, such as a triple-balance beam scale, or an electronic digital scale. Less specific, but still fairly accurate, measurements can be made on a kitchen scale, postage scale, or plastic balance scale.

vary from one color to the next. This happens because every color of every dyestuff has a somewhat different volume; for example, a teaspoon of yellow does not weigh exactly the same amount as a teaspoon of blue. In order to get stock solutions of precisely equal concentration, you would have to put the same *weight* of dye into each solution. Although this difference in concentration is quite real, it causes no problems for the home dyer, because you need a system which is repeatable more than you need a system in which all colors have equal concentration when they are in stock solutions.*

We have concluded that the advantages of the teaspoon system of measuring powdered dyes far outweigh the disadvantages. We have written the instructions for mixing stock solutions for all the dyestuffs used in this book with the teaspoon as our dye-measuring unit. In addition, we use teaspoons, tablespoons, and cups as volume measures for the dry chemicals.

We switch to the metric system for all liquid measures, however. This is because the most crucial measurement made in controlled dyeing is the measure of the *amount of dye stock solution* in the dyepot. It is easier and more accurate to measure tiny amounts of liquid using milliliters than to estimate fractions of teaspoons. In addition, metric calculations are arithmetically simple.**

This distinction between the measuring system used for the dry ingredients and that used for the liquid ingredients works very well, in spite of the apparent contradiction. No switching between the two systems is required as long as the dry ingredients are always measured with the English system, and the liquids are always measured with the metric system.† The consistency required for accurate controlled dyeing is retained.

Equipment for controlled dyeing

You will need to assemble the following basic tools and containers. Most are readily available at local stores. This equipment will be adequate for all the dyes covered in this book. Specific additional items will occasionally be required for special dye techniques, and these are listed with the projects.

Dyebath containers: You will need at least four containers if you plan to dye several colors at one time. For dyes that do not need to be heated you can use plastic pots or tubs. For dyes that require heat, use stainless steel, enamel-coated metal, or glass pots. Do not use pots

---

* The strength of your stock solution from one color to the next is not critically important. What is important is that you be able to mix each color to the same concentration as you have mixed that color before.

In fact, the dyestuffs, even when measured by weight, have intrinsically different values. The section on color mixing, in Chapter 6, offers more information on these differences and how to adjust for them.

** There's an additional benefit to the metric system; the measurement of weight (grams) is equivalent to the measurement of volume (ml), since 1 ml of water weighs 1 gram at room temperature.

†When working in the metric system it is easiest to stay with the metric measurements and not convert back and forth between the metric and English systems. However, a conversion chart is offered in the appendix.

made of metals which can interact with the dyes and chemicals, such as aluminum or iron. Each pot should hold at least two gallons of water for the average dye run. If you find you want to dye samples or small amounts, you may also want smaller containers.

Measuring and mixing equipment: You will need the following basic tools for measuring and mixing dyes and chemicals. It should be possible to obtain all the items at your local grocery, discount, and drug stores:

A set of plastic teaspoons
Measuring cups or containers, sized to measure 50
*   ml to 500 ml*
A 2-liter measure (for example, a soft-drink bottle)
Syringes to measure 0 ml to 1.0 ml, and 0 ml to 10 ml
Stir sticks of glass, stainless steel, plastic, or wood
Wide-mouth jars with lids, to be used for dye stock
*   solutions*

Mixing the dye stock solutions

Dyestuffs are mixed into stock solutions for two important reasons. First, the dye is easier to measure accurately; second, the dye is safer to use once it has been mixed into water. Since dye powder is easily airborne and dye liquid stays put better, working with liquids keeps your work space neater and minimizes the chance that you may breathe in any powder. In addition, powders occasionally cause allergic reactions.

When you mix stock solutions you must handle the dye powders briefly, and care is required. Wearing a respirator or dust mask is essential. A few other simple measures will help you control the powder. The best place to measure dye is in an enamel (not fiberglass) bathtub, because the area can be easily washed. If this is not possible, use a surface covered with several layers of newspapers in a well-lit area of the kitchen or basement. If you dampen the papers with a spray bottle of water, escaped dye will adhere to the paper rather than drift around. You can also control the dye by working in a box, dishpan, or five-gallon bucket turned on its side.

A stock solution is a measured amount of dye dissolved in a specific amount of water. Most dye instructions will contain a suggested stock solution concentration, which is expressed as a percentage of dye to water. For example, fiber-reactive dyes are usually mixed in a 2% solution. This means that 2 grams of dye are dissolved in 100 milliliters of water. In our teaspoon system, the percent concentration of the stock solutions is necessarily approximate. In Chapter 4, we list the teaspoon measures for stock solutions for each class of dyes.

Take care when mixing dye powders. After they are in solution, they are safer and easier to handle.

Measure the dye powder and put it into one of your measuring cups.

Add a small amount of your measured quantity of water.

Mix the dye powder and water to form a paste, so that all the powder is wet.

Add the rest of the measured water and stir well.

GENERAL PROCEDURES FOR MIXING A STOCK SOLUTION

You will use the following equipment for measuring, mixing, and storing your stock solutions:

- *Two measuring cups with metric divisions, capacity 500 ml*
- *A set of plastic measuring spoons*
- *A plastic or stainless metal rod or spoon for stirring*
- *A dust mask or respirator*
- *Jars with lids for storing stock solutions, one per color of dye*
- *Stick-on labels to date and identify stock solutions*

1. Measure the required number of teaspoons of dye into one measuring cup. Allow the dye to settle for a minute before you move it.

2. With your other measuring cup, measure the required amount of hot water. Use a small amount of this water to mix the dye into a paste, as if mixing a flour paste for gravy. If the dye does not mix easily, add a few drops of liquid detergent.

3. When the dye is smoothly pasted, gradually add the remainder of the measured water. Stir to mix the dye, and to wash off any dye on the mixing rod or spoon. Pour the dye into a storage bottle, rinse the measuring equipment, and proceed to the next color.

Most dye stock solutions have a shelf life; this means that they become less powerful the longer they are kept in liquid form. It is best to mix only the amount of stock solution that you will need at one time. If you do store stock solutions, date and label them carefully and keep them in a cool, dark place, away from food and out of the reach of children. Fiber-reactive dyes and union dyes can be stored for up to two months; acid dyes and pre-metallized dyes can be stored for up to six months without a noticeable loss of strength. Stock solutions that are past their prime can be successfully used to dye fiber, but don't trust them for controlled results.

Quantities of dye, water, and chemical assistants

Every dyebath contains a certain amount of water, dye, and sometimes chemical assistants. The single most important concept of controlled dyeing is: **The amount of each of the components of any dyebath is figured in relation to the weight of the fiber in that dyebath.**

How much dye?

The ratio of the amount of dye in the pot to the amount of fiber in the pot is the most important factor in determining the outcome of a dye run. For example, refer to the first four dyed colors for Project 1. You measured gradually smaller amounts of dye into the successive pots, so the color in each pot was paler than the color in the pot before. In each pot the quantity of material being dyed was the same, the dye color was the same, and the amount of dyeing time was the same. (The dye being used did not require any chemical assistants.) The only difference between the four colors was the amount of dye in each pot.

This leads to the second important concept of controlled dyeing: **The more dye applied to a given amount of material, the darker the resulting color.** With each class of dye, the scale for pale-to-dark will vary, but as a general rule (using stock solutions as indicated in Chapter 4), the following amounts of dye produce the following intensities on 100 grams of fiber:

pale shade — *1 to 2 ml dye*
light shade — *10 ml dye*
medium shade — *50 ml dye*
dark shade — *200 ml dye*

The familiar words *pale, light,* and so forth, differentiate the range.*

Water and chemical assistants

As mentioned above, the amounts of water and chemical assistants are also calculated with respect to the weight of the material being dyed. You need just enough water for the dye to circulate in the pot and reach the material. If there is too much water, the dye will be too spread out and will not find the fiber. *The typical ratio for water-to-fiber is 30 parts water to 1 part fiber.* For example, in a dyebath of 200 grams of fiber, 6000 ml (30 × 200 ml, or 6 liters) of water are required.

Dyestuffs require chemical assistants to fix the dye evenly to the fibers. These assistants are essential for colorfast dyeing, and each chemical has a specific function in the dyebath.

A **leveling agent** slows the movement of the dye onto the fiber and encourages the dye to spread evenly. Leveling agents are some form of salt. For most dyes, common household salt, sodium chloride (in plain or iodized form), is used. Some dyes require Glauber's salt, sodium sulfate. In some types of dyebaths, the salt also promotes movement of the dye onto the fiber, thus clearing or exhausting the dyebath.

A **fixer** helps the dye adhere, or bond, to the fiber. The fixer is either a mild acid (for protein fibers), or a mild alkali (for cellulose fibers).

The fixer for dyeing wool with fiber-reactive dyes, acid dyes, and pre-metallized dyes is acetic acid, which is available in 5% form as white vinegar. The fixer for dyeing cotton with fiber-reactive dyes is sodium carbonate, also known as sal soda, soda ash, or washing soda. Do not use the laundry-grade washing soda, which also

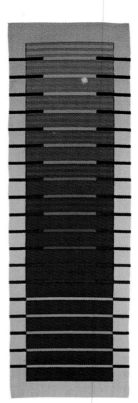

Ladder *by Budd Stalnaker*

---

*In the dye industry, the intensity of a color is expressed as a ratio of the quantity of dye to the weight of goods. This is known as the *depth of dye* (D.O.D.), and is written as a percentage. A 2% D.O.D. means that 2 grams of dye have been applied to 100 grams of fiber. The greater the depth of dye, the more dye per dyepot and the more intense the color.

The precision of the percentage values used in the dye industry is unnecessary for a personal controlled dye system.

contains whiteners and brighteners. Dye and chemical suppliers sell plain washing soda; some dye suppliers are listed in the appendix.

For each different type and brand of dye, the suggested ratio of chemical assistants to fiber will vary. In fact, different manufacturers and distributors supply different instructions for the same types of dyes. For controlled dyeing it is important to be consistent and stick to one recipe, but it doesn't matter which recipe you choose.

The dye recipes in Chapter 4 list the types and amounts of chemical assistants we suggest for each dye type. As mentioned above, the quantities of dry ingredients are expressed using the teaspoon system.

Recordkeeping

An important advantage of controlled dyeing is that it allows you to repeat your colors. If you keep a record of each dye run you can re-create a color on the same fiber with nearly exact dye lot matches. Re-creating a given color on another fiber will produce a color which is similar to the original, but not exactly the same. If you keep records and samples from each dye run you will build an invaluable reference file for creating colors in the future.

A dye record sheet can serve as a handy recipe during your dye run, and also provides your file copy. We have designed a record sheet to match our master recipes (see Chapter 4) as far as possible. This should make it easy for you to transfer the specific amounts that you need for your dye run from the master recipe to your individual record sheet. We recommend that you make multiple copies of this record sheet, or devise your own, and use it with every dye run. If you are running several dyepots at the same time, put a record sheet beside each dyebath to help keep track of the progress of that dyebath. Later, when the fibers are dry, attach a sample of the dyed fiber to the record sheet, and file it for future reference. If you have tied your skein with scraps of different types of yarn, you can also attach these to the record sheet.

Accurate records let you repeat your colors, and they serve as recipe cards to follow during dye runs.

DYE RECORD SHEET

Dye Recipe for _____ dye.   Date: _____

Mixing the Stock Solution: Use _____ tsp of dye per 100 ml water.
Mix according to instructions in Chapter 3.

TOTAL AMOUNT OF DYE PER POT:

Amount of fiber	Amount of dye
_____ gm	Color A _____
	Color B _____
	Color C _____
	Color D _____ Total dye per pot _____

AMOUNT OF ASSISTANTS PER POT:

Amount of fiber	Leveling agent(s)	Fixer(s)	Water (in liters)
_____ gm	_____ tsp	_____ tsp or ml	_____

THE DYE RUN

Step 1: Fill in the blanks above with the amounts of each ingredient. *Remember that the amounts of dye, assistants, and water depend on the quantity of fiber being dyed. The amount of fiber is listed twice, as a reminder.* **Prepare the dyepot** as follows:

—add water
—add leveling agent(s)
—stir well
—other: _____

Step 2: Add the dye and stir well.

Step 3: Leveling stage. Stir frequently. *For cellulose fibers,* stir for _____ minutes. *For protein fibers,* place dyepots on stove and bring gradually to a simmer (or 190° F for silk) during the next _____ minutes.

Step 4: Add fixer. Remove fiber from dyepot, add _____ tsp powdered fixer (previously dissolved in a small amount of water) or _____ ml liquid fixer. Stir well, then return fiber to the dyepot. Continue to stir frequently for the next _____ minutes to evenly distribute the fixer on the fiber.

Step 5: Cool down. *For protein fibers,* remove the dyepot from the heat and allow it to cool to room temperature. *For cellulose fibers,* proceed to step 6.

Step 6: Wash. Remove fiber from dyepot. Rinse it thoroughly in warm water until water runs clear. Wash gently with mild detergent and rinse again. Line dry.

Project 2: Eight-Value Hippari Jacket. *Eight different shades of black and an easy quilting technique make this sophisticated-looking jacket, which is actually simple to make.*

Project 2: Eight-Value Hippari Jacket

designed, dyed, and constructed by Kathryn Kreider

This project will introduce you to the measuring equipment and dyeing procedures described in Chapter 3. We will dye eight different shades of black, from a pale gray to a dark charcoal gray, using fiber-reactive dyes on 100% cotton fabric. Since the fiber-reactive dyes do not require heat on cotton fabric, we can run all eight dyepots at the same time. If you feel hesitant about managing all eight dyepots at once, do two dye runs with four dyepots in each, instead.

We will mix a stock solution from powdered black dye and use the syringes and measuring cups to measure exact quantities of the dye into our eight different pots. When our colors are done, we will make a multi-shade hippari jacket using strip-piecing techniques.

Equipment you will need:

- eight plastic pots to hold at least 2 gallons each (stainless steel, glass, or enamel will also work)
- plastic measuring spoons
- one 10-ml syringe
- one measuring cup with metric divisions, capacity at least 250 ml
- dishwashing gloves
- laundry (waterproof) marker

Materials you will need:

- one package (1 ounce) black fiber-reactive dye
- 4 ounces of fixer (sodium carbonate)
- ½ cup (¼ pound) regular or iodized salt
- 4 yards of 100% cotton fabric, width 44″–45″, cut into ½-yard pieces. If your fabric is of average weight, each piece will weigh approximately 50 grams. As long as each of your eight pieces is the same size, the exact weight does not matter.
- Folkwear Pattern #112, Japanese Field Clothing

Preparing the materials:

Using the laundry marker, number the fabric pieces 1 through 8. You will place each numbered fabric in its appropriate pot, with number 1 being the lightest value, and number 8 being the darkest. Wash the fabric pieces, and leave to wet out while you prepare the stock solution and the dyepots.

Preparing the dye:

Mix 350 ml of stock solution. Use 3½ tsp dye in 350 ml water (see page 22).

Preparing the dyepots:

Arrange all eight dyepots on a protected surface in your work area. Pour 1000 ml of water into each. Add 5 tsp of salt to each dyepot. Now measure dye into the pots according to the following recipe (see page 29):

Pot 1—1.25 ml dye
Pot 2—2.5 ml dye
Pot 3—5 ml dye
Pot 4—10 ml dye
Pot 5—20 ml dye
Pot 6—40 ml dye
Pot 7—80 ml dye
Pot 8—160 ml dye

The dye run:

Stir each dyebath. Add one piece of wet fabric to each dyebath. Stir frequently for 15 minutes. Be sure to lift and rotate the fabric to distribute the dye evenly.

Add the fixer at the 15-minute mark: for each dyepot mix 2 tsp of fixer (sodium carbonate) into a small amount of hot water. Stir to dissolve the fixer. Working with one dyepot at a time, remove the fabric from the dyebath, add the fixer solution, and return the fabric to the dyebath. Repeat until the fixer has been added to all eight pots. Continue to stir the pots frequently for the next 15 minutes, then stir occasionally for another 30 minutes. Total time for the dye run is one hour.

Remove the fabric from the dyepots, rinse thoroughly until the rinse water runs clear. Wash the fabric in mild detergent, rinse again and hang to dry.

Cut the six middle-value pieces into strips and sew them into rectangles that shade from light to dark. Cut two of these squares to make strips of diagonal stripes (see page 28).

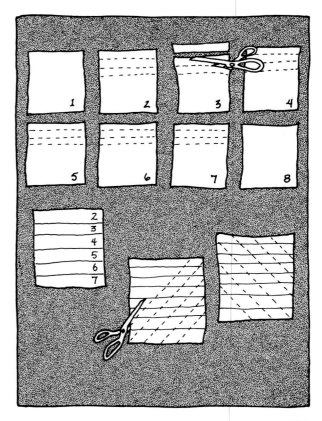

Constructing the hippari:

The strip-piecing construction technique used is known as Seminole patchwork. It is an economical and effective way to create rectangular and diagonal patchwork patterns.

Iron the fabric pieces, adjusting to straighten the grain. Set aside the darkest value for the front band, and reserve the lightest value for the large solid areas. The remaining six values are strip-pieced, using the value steps in order, as follows:

Tear or cut three 1¾″ strips of each color.

Stitch together 3 rectangles, each of which is constructed by assembling the six middle value steps (numbers 2–7) of gray, in order from light to dark.

Press the seams toward the darker colors.

Cut diagonal strips from two of these three pieced fabrics. Use a straightedge and a rotary cutter, or carefully draw the lines with tailor's chalk and cut with scissors. Cut into strips 1½″ wide, at a 45° angle. Cut the second fabric into 1½″-wide strips at a 45° angle in the opposite direction (see figures A and B below). Wait to cut your third pieced fabric until you know which of the 45° angles you require.

A variety of interesting patterns can be made when reassembling the strips. You will need to assemble your strips so as to construct fabric pieces which are large enough for and shaped to accommodate the hippari pattern pieces. Use the reserved lightest value as required for solid areas, and the darkest value for the front band. Cut the reserved pieced fabric as required to complete your pattern.

For a neatly finished hippari, line the jacket with a matching or contrasting fabric.

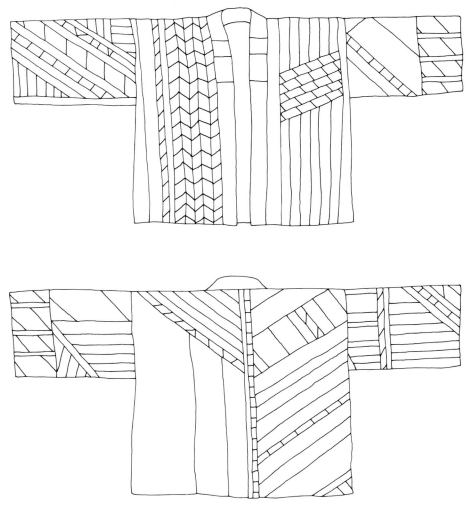

Assemble the strips of eight colors to make pieces of the right shape for the jacket pattern. Kathryn used the darkest value for the front band and the lightest value for the large solid areas. Follow her design or make up your own.

USING THE MEASURING SYRINGES

Small amounts of dye stock solution are accurately measured with the 10-ml plastic syringes. The barrel of a 10-ml syringe is marked in ½-ml steps. The rubber-tipped plunger both marks the amount of dye and ejects the dye. For accurate measurements, the lower rubber ring of the plunger tip should be level with the top edge of the volume mark required.

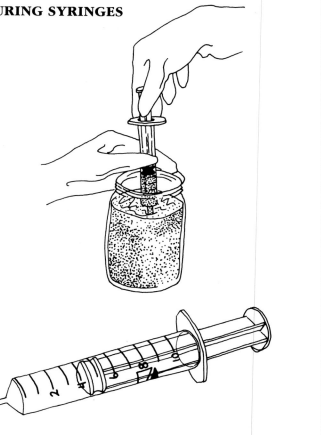

For example, to measure 5 ml of dye stock solution, first push the plunger to the 0 position. Insert the tip of the syringe into the dye solution. Gradually pull the plunger out to fill the syringe. If there are air bubbles in the syringe, empty the syringe while you hold its tip in the dye solution, and fill again. Align the lower ring of the plunger with the 5-ml line for an accurate 5-ml volume measurement. Push the plunger to eject the dye into your dyepot. To measure quantities of dye solution smaller than ½ ml, use a smaller syringe which holds a total of 1 ml, with 1/10-ml graduations.

4

Choosing the Right Dyestuff

Dyestuffs are categorized by the types of fiber they will dye. Each fiber type has a different chemical structure, and therefore requires a separate kind of dye. There are many different kinds of dyes, divided into classes depending on the fibers they will dye and the chemical assistants they require. For example, the *acid dyes* are a class of dyes for wool which use an acid as a fixer. Of the many classes of dyes, only the few which are suitable for home use will be considered in this book. These types of dye are more than adequate for the needs of the average textile craftsperson. The only limitation is that none of these dyes is capable of dyeing most synthetic fibers. That is because the dyes for synthetic fibers are either too complicated or too hazardous to be adapted for home dyeing. The dyes that are included in this book are man-made, or *synthetic*, dyes which will dye *natural* fibers. To be able to choose which dye will work best for you, you will need to have a working knowledge of the classes of dyes and the types of fibers they will dye.

Fiber types

The first step in selecting a dye is to determine the type of fiber you will be dyeing. There are **three groups of fibers:** the animal, or *protein*, fibers; the plant, or *cellulose*, fibers; and the man-made, or *synthetic*, fibers.

Protein fibers

Protein fibers are all, except for silk, obtained from the hair or fur of animals. Well-known protein fibers include wool, alpaca, angora, and mohair. Protein fibers are noted for their warmth, durability, flame-resistance, and wrinkle-resistance. They can be harmed by strong chemical or physical treatment, and need to be washed with care. Bleach and harsh detergents can damage the fiber; excessive agitation or sudden changes in temperature can cause dramatic shrinking and felting.

Silk is a secretion of the silkworm, and has special characteristics. It is a smooth continuous fiber with a natural luster in its filament form. Silk is prized for its strength and its draping qualities.

Many of the protein fibers are considered to be luxury fibers in today's market. The rarest fibers, such as cashmere, angora, qiviut, and silk, are particularly valuable. There are degrees of quality within each protein fiber type, depending on the length, or staple, of the fiber, and the breed and age of the animal producing the fiber. The different types of protein fibers are listed on page 32.

Cellulose fibers

Cellulose fibers are obtained from plants. The most familiar cellulose fiber, cotton, is a *seed* fiber. Mercerized cotton has been chemically treated to increase its luster and strength. Other familiar plant fibers, such as linen, jute, and ramie, are stem, or *bast*, fibers; raffia is a *leaf* fiber. All cellulose fibers are known for being

---

SAFETY GUIDELINES

The home dyer's use of industrial-strength dyes and chemicals has increased dramatically over the past twenty years. Coincidentally, consumers have also become more aware of the need to handle chemicals in a responsible manner which insures the safety of ourselves, our neighbors, and our environment. For every manufactured chemical, including every dyestuff, a *Material Safety Data Sheet* is provided by the manufacturer. These data sheets report the results of tests to determine the physical, health, fire, explosive, and reactivity hazard levels of the chemical in question. Most dye suppliers will provide a copy of a relevant data sheet, upon request.

Like most household chemicals, dyes and their assistant chemicals can be hazardous if carelessly or improperly used. Although the dyes are not toxins or poisons, ingestion and absorption of the dyes is to be avoided. The primary hazard from the dyes and chemicals is lung irritation from excessive inhalation of the particles or fumes. It is possible for a particular individual to be allergic to the dye powders or chemicals, and individuals who have tendencies toward allergies should proceed with extra caution.

The following guidelines constitute reasonable and appropriate measures to insure safe dyeing.

1. **Avoid inhaling dye** powders or fumes. If you use dyes occasionally, use an allergy dust mask when working with dye powders. If you use dyes frequently, you should obtain a NIOSH-approved respirator (one tested by the National Institute of Occupational Safety and Health).
2. **Protect your skin** (an easily dyed protein substance) by wearing rubber gloves.
3. **Wear protective clothing**, or have a set of "dye clothes" that remain in your dye area.

4. **Keep a separate set of dye equipment** which is never used for cooking, including dyepots, measuring and stirring equipment, and storage containers.
5. If possible, **establish a dye area** in your basement, garage, or studio. Avoid dyeing in your kitchen if you can. If you must dye in your kitchen, clean surfaces thoroughly and put all dye materials away when you are done.
6. **Don't eat, drink, or smoke** in your dye area.
7. **If you are pregnant,** or think you are pregnant, or are planning to be pregnant soon, **do not dye.**
8. **Carefully label** all dyes and chemicals and store them out of children's and pets' reach.
9. **Dispose of all dye solutions responsibly.** If you frequently dye large amounts of material, it is best to neutralize your dyebath solutions before dumping them out. Use baking soda to neutralize an acid bath, and vinegar to neutralize a basic bath.

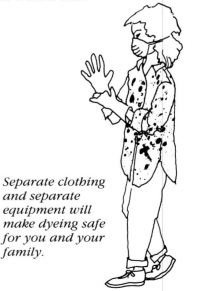

Separate clothing and separate equipment will make dyeing safe for you and your family.

absorbent, comfortable to wear in warm climates, and resistant to high-temperature treatments. The bast fibers are known for their strength, which is due to their long staple length. Among the disadvantages of cellulose fibers are their low resiliency (which leads to easy wrinkling), their flammability, and their moderately poor colorfastness. Most cellulose fibers are easily obtained and economical to produce, and therefore they have remained inexpensive and easy to obtain, in general. The more familiar cellulose fibers are listed in the chart.

Synthetic fibers

Synthetic fibers are man-made from chemical syrups, or resins, extruded through tiny holes to form continuous fibers. The fibers are then grouped together to make a long filament tow, or untwisted rope of fibers. This bundle of fibers is cut into short staple lengths and then spun into the final synthetic fiber product. Synthetic fibers were developed, starting with rayon, at the beginning of the twentieth century, to meet the need for inexpensive fibers. In general, synthetics are known not only for their strength, but also for their wrinkle-resistance and their ability to accommodate to modern detergents and washing machines. Most synthetic fibers are generated from petrochemical byproducts. They are usually dyed in the early stages of production when still in liquid form, since once they are extruded and spun they become resistant to the dye. Most synthetic fibers cannot be easily dyed at home, since the appropriate dyes are not readily available, are difficult to use, and require strong chemical assistants.

However, there are two synthetic fibers which *can* be dyed by the home dyer. *Rayon* is made from regenerated cellulose fiber from either wood or cotton. Rayon retains all the properties of natural cellulose fibers, so it is easily dyed using cellulose dyes and recipes. *Nylon* can sometimes by dyed with acid dyes. Actually there are many different "nylons," only some of which accept these dyes. The easiest way to determine if the nylon you have is dyeable is to try a small amount and see if the dye takes.

For our purposes it is important to list and identify the synthetic fibers along with the natural fibers, so you can avoid trying to dye those which are difficult. These fibers may occur singly or in blends with other fibers. Thus, the most well-known of the synthetic fibers are listed in the chart.

Because she dyed them herself, Kathryn had no trouble getting many color-coordinated fabrics for her Stella Rosella *quilt.*

Protein Fibers	Cellulose Fibers	Synthetic Fibers
wool	cotton	acetate
alpaca	linen (flax fiber)	nylon
llama	ramie	olefin
mohair	jute	Orlon® (acrylic)
angora	hemp	polyester
cashmere	sisal	acrylic
qiviut	raffia	Spandex®
silk	(viscose rayon)	

Burn testing

Occasionally you may want to dye a yarn or fabric of unknown composition. An easy method of testing for fiber type is known as a *burn test*. To test a fiber by this method you subject a small piece of the fiber to a direct flame, and observe the way it burns. You watch to see how fast it burns, what type of odor and smoke are created, and what sort of residue or ash remains afterwards. Some fibers burn quickly, so it is safest to use a reasonably large sample and to hold the sample with tweezers or burn it in a metal container.

Cellulose fibers burn quickly with a smell similar to that of burning wood or paper, produce a gray or white smoke, and leave a feathery gray ash.

Protein fibers burn slowly with a sharp smell like that of burning hair, and produce a dark smoke and a black, crushable ash.

Synthetic fibers burn with an acrid smell, and melt leaving a hard pellet residue rather than an ash.

If a fiber burn test appears inconclusive because the fiber exhibits a combination of these characteristics the sample is probably a blend of fibers.

View Out Back *by Anneke Herrold*

Classes of dyes

We will discuss four different classes of dyes in this book:

- *union dyes* (sometimes called *household dyes*)
- *fiber-reactive dyes* (powdered form and liquid form)
- *acid dyes*
- *pre-metallized dyes*

These dyes are all currently available for purchase by the home dyer. Each type is easy to use and to store, and provides a wide range of colors. Each is suitable for controlled dyeing and a variety of applications. All of the dyestuffs will dye natural fibers only, with the exception of some union dyes which yield pale colors on synthetic fibers or blends.

Each different class of dyes has its own color range and its own characteristics, which make it suitable for some uses and not for others. It is important to note that there is no single dye which will produce optimal results on all fiber types. Some dyes will dye only very specific fiber types. Others may dye many types of fibers, but are not as lightfast or washfast. Under our guidance, you will experiment with the different classes of dyes, and learn to choose the one which best fits your individual needs.

An understanding of the different classes of dyes is made more complicated by the wide variety of dyestuffs and dye names on the market. Although there are fewer than twenty major dye manufacturers in the world, there are many more dye repackagers. The final packages often carry the repackager's trade name, instead of the dye's original trade name or generic name. In our discussion of the dye classes, we use generic rather than trade names. The various trade names, as well as many of the secondary repack names, for the classes of dyes in this book are listed in the appendix.

Applying dye

Usually the instructions provided with dyestuffs are for immersion-type dyeing. This is the procedure in which the fiber is completely immersed in a solution of dye and assistants for a specified length of time. Besides the important chemicals discussed in Chapter 3, the other factors which determine the effectiveness of a dye's bond to the fiber during an immersion dye run are the **amount of heat supplied**, the **speed at which the heat is increased** during the dye run, and the **total duration** of the dye run.

As we have mentioned, there are ways to apply dyes other than the familiar immersion technique. Most of these involve direct application of the dyes. With these techniques the dyes can be used like paints to achieve multicolored designs on a single piece of fiber or fabric. You can color fibers with either *dyes*, which we are discussing, or with *paints*, which are pigments applied to the surface of the fabric. The advantage of using dyes rather than textile paints is that the resulting fabric is supple rather than stiff, and the colors have the permanence of the dye being used. Since with direct application the fibers are not immersed for a significant period of time in a dye and fixer solution, alternate methods for ensuring that the dyes adhere to the fibers have been developed for most dyestuffs. A discussion of some of these different application procedures appears in Chapter 7.

Other techniques we will discuss are *overdyeing* and *double-dyeing* (Chapter 8). With these methods, fibers are dyed once and then re-dyed, to get different effects. Some dyes can be used in this way and some cannot. A **non-reversible dyestuff** is one whose dye molecules bond to the fiber so firmly that they do not release when the fiber is immersed in another dyebath. In practice this means that the dyes from the first dye run will not bleed into the dyepot on the second run. A **reversible dyestuff**, on the other hand, will bleed into subsequent dyebaths and the first run's colors will "pollute" those of the second run, causing muddy and poorly differentiated color results.

Four dyes for the home dyer

Union dyes

The most commonly available dye, which can usually be found in grocery stores, dime stores, or craft shops, is known as union or household dye. This type of dye is designed to work on most fibers, including some synthetics, although significantly paler results occur on synthetic fibers than on natural fibers. The reason that these dyes can be so versatile is that each package of dye actually contains several different classes of dyes mixed together. When you use a household dye, only the dye that is appropriate for the fiber that you put in the pot will be absorbed. The other dyestuffs will remain in the dyepot liquid and be discarded at the end of the dye run.

Union dyes can be used for immersion dyeing, direct application such as painting and stenciling, and for staining wood and paper. They are usually reversible, and therefore cannot be used for over-dyeing and double-dyeing (see Chapter 8).

Union or household dyes do not require an assistant other than salt, and often the salt comes mixed with the dye. Union dyes are absorbed by the fiber, but will not form a firm bond to it. As a result, the color will not be particularly lightfast or washfast.

These dyes are useful because they are so easy to get. They are ideal for quick projects that do not require permanence, such as children's clothing soon to be outgrown, costumes, and so forth. They are not highly recommended for projects that will be subject to bright sunlight or frequent washing.

Fiber-reactive dyes

Fiber-reactive dyes are the newest class of dyes, having been developed in 1956. They are versatile and very permanent, with a well-deserved popularity. They are used industrially for clothing because they have very high ratings for washfastness and lightfastness. They are called *reactive* because they chemically react with the fiber and form a permanent bond with it. Fiber-reactive dyes can be used for immersion dyeing, for direct application such as painting or spraying, and for screen, block, or stamp printing. They are a non-reversible dyestuff and are excellent for overdyeing and double-dyeing.

There are several different types of fiber-reactive dyes. All of them are so similar that the different types can be used together in a project or even in a single dyepot with good results. A liquid form of fiber-reactive dyes has recently been developed, which eliminates the need to mix stock solutions. It is more expensive than the powdered form and is therefore impractical for large projects. This dye is particularly suitable for surface design techniques and will be discussed in further detail in Chapter 7.

Fiber-reactive dyes are a uniquely comprehensive class of dyes. *These are the dyes to choose if you plan to stock only one type of dye and want to be able to dye a variety of natural fibers.* They were designed for use on cellulose fibers, with salt and sodium carbonate (washing soda) as the chemical assistants. However, fiber-reactive dyes can also be used on protein fibers, with salt and mild acetic acid (white vinegar) as the assistants. Manufacturers often do not mention that fiber-reactive dyes work well on protein fibers when used in an acid solution, but do not let that inhibit you. Just follow the directions in this chapter. Silk can also be dyed, using either the cellulose or the protein recipe. The reactive dyes will not dye synthetic fibers other than rayon.

Acid dyes

Acid dyes are specifically designed for protein fibers. They require acid for the dye to be effective, and also heat to fix the dye onto the fiber.

Acid dyes are most often used for immersion dyeing, but can also be applied with surface design techniques on silk and wool. They are ideal for rainbow dye techniques. They produce vivid colors on wool and silk. Acid dyes are reversible and cannot be used for over-dyeing or double-dyeing.

There are three types of acid dyes, distinguished from each other by the strength of the acid bath required to fix them: strong, weak, and neutral. The most readily available acid dye for the home dyer is the strong, or leveling, acid dye. Strong acid dyes are also known as "Kiton" acid dyes. Commercially, they are fixed with strong acids such as hydrochloric or sulfuric acid, which are much too hazardous for home use. Good results can be obtained by substituting the milder acetic acid. Since 5% acetic acid is sold in the grocery store as white vinegar, this substitution proves to be very practical. The only disadvantage with the weaker acid is that not all of the dye is exhausted (taken up by the fiber), so that some fraction of the available dye is wasted. The advantages of storing and using the mild acid far outweigh this disadvantage. It is best to use a name-brand white vinegar, rather than a generic or house brand, because the name brands are more consistent in strength and have a longer shelf life. If you do a lot of acid dyeing you may want to obtain a more concentrated solution of acetic acid. You can buy 28% and 56% acetic acids from photo-supply shops and dye-chemical suppliers. Although many recipes for acid dyes call for Glauber's salt, regular table salt may be used instead.

Pre-metallized dyes

These dyes are a combination of an acid dye and a metal salt mordant (a special chemical assistant). They produce brilliant colors on protein fibers, and provide a different color range from that of the acid dyes. They can be used for immersion dyeing and direct application techniques. The pre-metallized dyes are non-reversible and can be used with good results for overdyeing and double-dyeing.

This class of dyes requires more precise control, extra chemical assistants, and more time per dye run than the acid and reactive dyes. Two salts and two acids are used to adjust the dyebath. However, the pre-metallized dyes are concentrated, so that a very little dye goes a long way. In addition, these dyes completely exhaust in the dyebath, so that no dye is wasted.

DYE RECIPE
Union Dye

MIXING THE STOCK SOLUTION: Use 1 package dry dye per 100 ml water, mixed according to instructions in Chapter 3, or use pre-mixed liquid dye. (*Note: a bottle of liquid dye contains approximately 200 ml stock solution.*)

TOTAL AMOUNT OF DYE PER POT

Amount of Fiber (in grams)	Amount of Dye (in milliliters)			
	Dark	*Medium*	*Light*	*Pale*
500	250	125	50	25
200	100	50	20	10
100	50	25	10	5
50	25	12	5	2.5
10	5	2.5	1	0.5

AMOUNT OF ASSISTANTS PER POT

Amount of Fiber (in grams)	Amount of Water (in liters except last entry)
500	15
200	6
100	3
50	1.5
10	300 ml

Note: the salt for these dyes is usually mixed in with the dye. If not, follow instructions on the dye package.

THE DYE RUN

Total time = 60 minutes plus cool down, if heated. Use the charts above to determine the amount of each ingredient. Remember the amounts of dye and water depend on the quantity of fiber. Wash and wet out your fibers.

Step 1: Place _____ ml **hot water** in the dyepot.

Step 2: Add the **dye**, stir well, and place wet fiber in the pot.

   Color A _____ ml
   Color B _____ ml
   Color C _____ ml
   Total dye _____ ml

Steps 3–4: Leveling stage. Stir frequently for 30 to 45 minutes. *For darker colors,* place the dyepots on stove and bring gradually to a simmer over the next 15 minutes. Continue to simmer, stirring frequently for the next 30 minutes.

Step 5: Cool down. If dyepot was heated, remove dyepot from heat and allow to cool to room temperature. If not, proceed to Step 6.

Step 6: Wash. Remove fiber from pot, rinse thoroughly in warm water until water runs clear. Wash gently with mild detergent and rinse again. Line dry.

DYE RECIPE
Fiber-Reactive Dye (Cellulose)

MIXING THE STOCK SOLUTION: Use 1 tsp of dye per 100 ml water, mixed according to instructions in Chapter 3.

TOTAL AMOUNT OF DYE PER POT

Amount of Fiber (in grams)	Amount of Dye (in milliliters)			
	Dark	*Medium*	*Light*	*Pale*
500	1000	250	50	10
200	400	100	20	4
100	200	50	10	2
50	100	25	5	1
10	20	5	1	0.2

AMOUNT OF ASSISTANTS PER POT

Amount of Fiber (in grams)	Leveling agent (salt, in tsp)	Fixer (soda, in tsp)	Water (in liters, except last entry)
500	50 (1 c)	20 (½ c)	15
200	20 (½ c)	8 (3 T)	6
100	10 (¼ c)	4	3
50	5 (2 T)	2	1.5
10	1	½	300 ml

THE DYE RUN

Total time = 45–60 minutes. Use the charts above to determine the amount of each ingredient. Remember the amounts of dye, assistants, and water depend on the quantity of fiber. Wash and wet out your fibers.

Step 1: Prepare the dyepot as follows:
   add water: _____ liters
   add salt: _____
   Stir well.

Step 2: Add the **dye**, stir well, and place wet fiber in the pot.
   Color A _____ ml
   Color B _____ ml
   Color C _____ ml
   Total dye _____ ml

Step 3: Leveling stage. Stir frequently for 15 minutes.

Step 4: Add **fixer.** Remove fiber from dyepot, add _____ tsp soda (dissolve soda in a small amount of water before adding it), stir well, return fiber to the dyepot. Continue to stir frequently for the next 30–45 minutes to evenly distribute the fixer on the fiber.

Step 5: (optional). *For dark colors,* leave the fiber to dye longer, several hours or overnight (no stirring is necessary).

Step 6: Wash. Remove fiber from pot, rinse thoroughly in warm water until water runs clear. Wash gently with mild detergent and rinse again. Line dry.

DYE RECIPE
Fiber-Reactive Dye (Protein)

MIXING THE STOCK SOLUTION: Use 1 tsp of dye per 100 ml water, mixed according to instructions in Chapter 3.

TOTAL AMOUNT OF DYE PER POT

Amount of Fiber (in grams)	Amount of Dye (in milliliters)			
	Dark	*Medium*	*Light*	*Pale*
500	1000	250	50	10
200	400	100	20	4
100	200	50	10	2
50	100	25	5	1
10	20	5	1	0.2

AMOUNT OF ASSISTANTS PER POT

Amount of Fiber (in grams)	Leveling agent (salt, in tsp)	Fixer (vinegar, in ml)	Water (in liters, except last entry)
500	25 (½ c)	500	15
200	10 (¼ c)	200	6
100	5 (2 T)	100	3
50	3 (1 T)	50	1.5
10	½	10	300 ml

THE DYE RUN

Total time = 45–60 minutes plus cool down. Use the charts above to determine the amount of each ingredient. Remember the amounts of dye, assistants, and water depend on the quantity of fiber. Wash and wet out your fibers.

Step 1: Prepare the dyepot as follows:

    add water: _____ liters
    add salt: _____
    Stir well.

Step 2: Add the **dye**, stir well, and place wet fiber in the pot.

    Color A _____ ml
    Color B _____ ml
    Color C _____ ml
    Total dye _____ ml

Step 3: Leveling stage. *(Note: No heat is required for silk fibers.)* For other protein fibers, place the dyepots on stove and bring gradually to a simmer over a period of 15 minutes, stirring frequently.

Step 4: Add **fixer.** Remove fiber from dyepot, add _____ ml fixer and stir well. Return fiber to the dyepot. Continue to stir frequently for the next 30–45 minutes to evenly distribute the fixer on the fiber.

Step 5: Cool down. Remove dyepot from heat and allow to cool gradually to room temperature. *For darker shades,* leave several hours or overnight.

Step 6: Wash. Remove fiber from pot, rinse thoroughly in warm water until water runs clear. Wash gently with mild detergent and rinse again. Line dry.

DYE RECIPE
Acid Dye

MIXING THE STOCK SOLUTION: Use ½ tsp of dye per 100 ml water. Mix according to instructions in Chapter 3.

TOTAL AMOUNT OF DYE PER POT

Amount of Fiber (in grams)	Amount of Dye (in milliliters)			
	Dark	Medium	Light	Pale
500	1000	250	50	10
200	400	100	20	4
100	200	50	10	2
50	100	25	5	1
10	20	5	1	0.2

AMOUNT OF ASSISTANTS PER POT

Amount of Fiber (in grams)	Leveling agent (salt)	Fixer (in ml) (5% acetic (acid [vinegar])	Water (in liters)
500	5 T	250 (twice) = 500	15
200	2 T	100 (twice) = 200	6
100	1 T	50 (twice) = 100	3
50	1 ½ tsp	25 (twice) = 50	1 ½
10	½ tsp	5 (twice) = 10	½

THE DYE RUN
Total time = 60 minutes plus cool down. Use the charts above to determine the amount of each ingredient. Remember the amounts of dye, assistants, and water depend on the quantity of fiber. Wash and wet out your fibers.

Step 1: Prepare the dyepot as follows:
   add water: _____ liters
   add salt: _____
   Stir well.

Step 2: Add the **dye**, stir well, and place wet fiber in the pot.
   Color A _____ ml
   Color B _____ ml
   Color C _____ ml
   Total dye _____ ml

Step 3: Leveling stage. Stir frequently during this stage. Place the dyepots on stove and bring gradually to a simmer (or 190° F for silk) for the next 30 minutes.

Step 4: Add fixer. Remove fiber from dyepot, add _____ ml vinegar and stir well, return fiber to the dyepot. Continue to stir frequently for the next 15 minutes to evenly distribute the fixer on the fiber. Then remove the fiber again, add another _____ ml vinegar, return the fiber to the dyepot. Continue to stir occasionally and simmer for another 15 minutes.

Step 5: Cool down. Remove dyepot from heat and allow to cool gradually to room temperature. *For darker shades,* leave several hours or overnight.

Step 6: Wash. Remove fiber from pot, rinse thoroughly in warm water until water runs clear. Wash gently with mild detergent and rinse again. Line dry.

DYE RECIPE
Pre-Metallized Dye

MIXING THE STOCK SOLUTION: Use ½ tsp of dye per 100 ml water, mixed according to instructions in Chapter 3.

TOTAL AMOUNT OF DYE PER POT

Amount of Fiber (in grams)	Amount of Dye (in milliliters)			
	Dark	*Medium*	*Light*	*Pale*
500	1000	500	250	100
200	400	200	100	40
100	200	100	50	20
50	100	50	25	10
10	20	10	5	2

AMOUNT OF ASSISTANTS PER POT

Amount of Fiber (in grams)	Leveling agents		Fixers		Water (in liters)
	(Glauber's salt) (in tsp)	*(Albegel set) (in ml)*	*(sodium acetate) (in tsp)*	*(acetic acid) (in ml)*	
500	10 (3 T)	5	5	160	8
200	4	2	2	80	4
100	2	1	1	40	2
50	1	0.5	½	20	1
10	½	0.25	⅛	8	400 ml

THE DYE RUN

Total time = 75–95 minutes plus cool down. Use the charts above to determine the amount of each ingredient. Remember the amounts of dye, assistants, and water depend on the quantity of fiber. Wash and wet out your fibers.

Step 1: Prepare the dyepot as follows:

    add water: _____ liters
    add leveling agents:
       Glauber's salt _____
       Albegel set _____
    add fixers:
       sodium acetate _____
       acetic acid _____

Check pH level of the dyebath; it should equal 4.5 to 5.0. Stir well. Add wetted-out fiber, leave for 10 minutes, stirring occasionally.

Step 2: Remove the fiber from the pot, add the **dye**, stir well, and return the fiber to the pot.

    Color A _____ ml
    Color B _____ ml
    Color C _____ ml
    Total dye _____ ml

Step 3: Leveling stage. Stir frequently during this stage. Place the dyepots on stove and bring gradually to a simmer (or 190° F for silk) for the next 45 minutes.

Step 4: Continue to **simmer** (only 190° F for silk) and **stir** frequently for the next 20–30 minutes.

Step 5: Cool down. Remove dyepot from heat and allow to cool gradually to room temperature.

Step 6: Wash. Remove fiber from pot, rinse thoroughly in warm water until water runs clear. Wash gently with mild detergent and rinse again. Line dry.

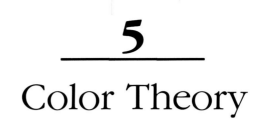

5
Color Theory

Mixing your own colors is easy. All you need is some practice with controlled dyeing and a basic understanding of color relationships. Most home dyers begin creating their own colors out of necessity. Dyes come in a range of premixed colors, with anywhere from 12 to 25 colors from which to choose. Often none of the colors is quite right, and it is necessary to mix two or more dye colors to obtain what you need. For example, suppose the shade of green you want contains more yellow than the dye mix offered by the manufacturer. You would buy both green and yellow dye, and add a bit of yellow to the green. You might need to dye several samples before you find the perfect combination. If you wanted to be able to create the same color of yellow-green again, you would keep a record of the exact amounts of each color that you used.

This combination of experimentation with measured amounts of dyestuffs and recordkeeping is all there is to creating your own colors. In order to economize on time and effort it is helpful to be able to predict the results of a two-color dye mix before beginning. Your records will help you, and the mastery of a few simple color facts is essential. The following discussion and the projects in this chapter illustrate basic color relationships.

The three qualities of a color which can be varied to create new colors are its *hue*, its *value*, and its *intensity*.

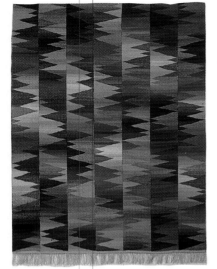

Tapis *by Diane Itter*

Hue

The hue of a color is the pure state of that color. Many hues have names; the most familiar hues are the **primary colors** of red, yellow, and blue. An equal mix of two primary colors creates the **secondary colors**: orange (red mixed with yellow), green (yellow mixed with blue), and purple (blue mixed with red). These six colors can be arranged in the traditional color wheel, with red, blue, and yellow at the points of an equilateral triangle, and the secondary colors between each pair of primaries. In addition, the **tertiary colors** can be inserted between each pair of secondary and primary colors, for a total of twelve basic hues. This process can be continued indefinitely, since theoretically there are an infinite number of hues which exist between any two hues on the color wheel.

The colors that are directly across from each other on the color wheel are called **complements**. Red is the complement of green, and vice versa; purple complements yellow, and blue complements orange. Two complementary colors can be used together to enliven a color composition. When two complements are juxtaposed in equal amounts, the brilliance of each color is heightened, and a visual

Evening Light *by Betsy Blumenthal*

vibration is created. If two complementary colors are used in unequal proportions the visual vibration is moderated, with a more harmonious but still exciting visual result. When two complementary colors are physically mixed, as when mixing pigments or dyes, a gray or brown color results.

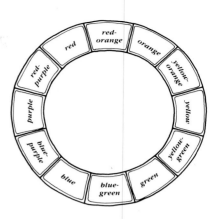

The twelve-step color wheel shows the primary, secondary, and tertiary colors.

Value

The value of a color refers to the light-to-dark range of that color. For example, pink is a light value and burgundy is a dark value of red. Using value gradations is an effective way to achieve the illusion of depth or dimensionality. Light color values also give the illusion of a light source coming from behind the composition. When mixing pigments for painting, a change in value of a color is achieved by adding white to lighten the hue or adding black to darken the hue. With dyes, a range of values of a given color hue is created by changing the amount of dye used on a given quantity of material. There is no "white" dye. The less dye used, the lighter the value; the more dye used, the darker the value. To obtain still darker values a small amount of black can be added.

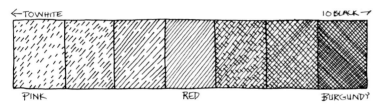

Value is the light-to-dark range of a color. The red value scale goes from pale pink to dark burgundy.

Intensity

The third color quality, that of intensity, also referred to as *saturation* or *vividness*, is the bright-to-dull range of a color. The brightest colors are the pure hues on the color wheel, and less intense colors are those which are grayer or browner. In color mixing with dye, the less intense colors are created by adding brown or black to a pure hue. Another way to achieve a less saturated color is to add small amounts of its complement, or the opposite color on the color wheel. For example, a small amount of green added to red will yield a rusty or brownish red, or a small amount of red added to green will yield an olive-green. An approximately equal mix of red and green will yield brown, the least saturated shade in the range between red and green. The use of these muted colors can help you create a harmonious composition. A less intense color can provide a background for a splash of intense color which appears brighter relative to its subdued environment.

43

The color sphere

The relationships among these three color qualities of hue, value, and intensity can be illustrated clearly with the three-dimensional diagram called the color sphere. The pure colors of the color wheel are placed at the equator of the color sphere. The value gradation of each hue extends in the vertical direction, with the palest value of a hue at the top of the sphere and the darkest value at the bottom. The intensity scale for a given hue extends radially from the center of the sphere, with the most brilliant colors on the outside of the sphere and the most saturated, least intense, colors at the center of the sphere.

All potential colors can be assigned to a position on the color sphere, and the relationships among the three color characteristics become obvious. Any *horizontal slice* through the color sphere will reveal a color family of related hues, all of a given value, with the most brilliant shade at the perimeter of the slice. A *wedge cut vertically* will yield a slice in the shape of an orange segment which will contain all the values and all the intensities for the given hue. A *diagonal pathway across the surface* of the sphere will yield a range of colors which change in hue and in value. A *diagonal pathway through the interior* of the sphere will yield a range of colors which change in hue, value, and intensity. The color sphere contains an infinite array of colors and by extension there is also an infinite number of paths around and through the sphere.

Project 3 takes a walk around the color wheel on the equator of the color sphere. We used a twelve-step method to create a rainbow of colors with this dye run. We then constructed two multicolor baby blankets or cotton throws—a knit version and a woven version. If you prefer fewer colors, follow the instructions for dyeing the primary and secondary colors to get a simpler six-step set of colors.

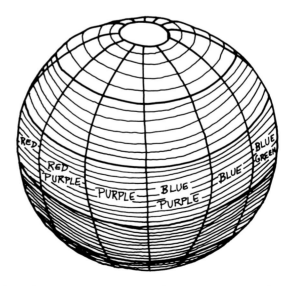

The relationships between hue, value, and intensity are shown by the color sphere. Pure hues of the color wheel are placed around the equator of the sphere.

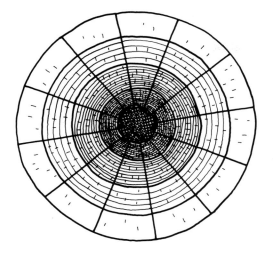

A horizontal slice will show all hues in the same value, with the most intense colors on the perimeter and grey in the center.

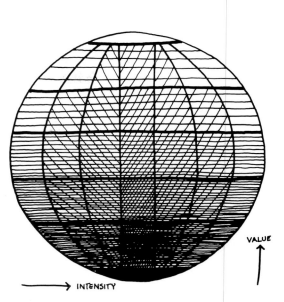

VALUE

INTENSITY

A vertical slice will show white at the top, black at the bottom, and different values of a pure hue shading from top to bottom. Horizontally across this slice, colors will change from pure at one side through grey at the center to a pure hue of the complementary color on the other side. The vertically cut wedge (either the lefthand or righthand half of the vertical slice) contains all the values and all the intensities for a single hue.

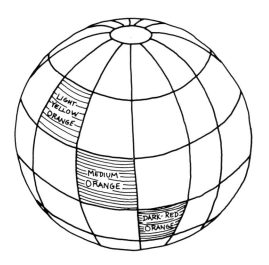

LIGHT YELLOW ORANGE

MEDIUM ORANGE

DARK RED ORANGE

A diagonal pathway across the surface of the sphere will show a range of colors which change in hue and value.

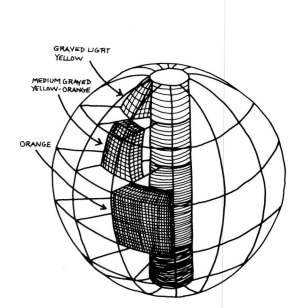

GRAYED LIGHT YELLOW

MEDIUM GRAYED YELLOW-ORANGE

ORANGE

A diagonal pathway through the interior of the sphere will yield a range of colors which change in hue, value, and intensity.

Project 3: Color Wheel Baby Blankets

designed, dyed, knit, and woven by Betsy Blumenthal

There is something very satisfying about using all twelve of the basic hues from the color wheel in a single piece. We succumbed to the urge and designed these cotton baby blankets for you to try. We decided on fiber-reactive dyes and cotton yarns or fabric because the dyes are easy to get and you don't need heat to set them on cotton; the ambitious dyer can run all twelve dyepots at once.

In the medium-dark value range, fiber-reactive dyes produce lively colors which said "baby" to us. If you prefer a more pastel version, use half as much dye in each pot. Where our instructions call for a total of 50 ml of dye per pot, check your pastel adjustments by being sure you will have a total of 25 ml of dye per pot. This is the amount required to produce a "medium" shade on 50 grams of cotton.

We've planned for you to dye enough cotton to knit or weave two 33" × 45" blankets. If you prefer, you can dye just six colors—the primaries and secondaries. In this case, you will have enough yarn for one average-sized woven or knit blanket.

Equipment you will need:
- six or twelve plastic (or other non-reactive) dyepots, capacity 2 gallons (the number depends on whether you will dye six or twelve colors)
- plastic measuring spoons
- three measuring cups with metric divisions, capacity of each at least 250 ml
- three 10-ml syringes
- three jars with lids, for storing stock solutions, capacity at least 300 ml
- dishwashing gloves
- stir sticks
- cardboard for winding skeins, 18" × 6"

Materials you will need:
- primary colors of fiber-reactive dye: ½ ounce each of red, yellow, and blue
- 2 cups (1 pound) salt
- 4 ounces fixer (sodium carbonate)
- 600 grams of 100% cotton flake yarn, with about 110 yards/ounce, for twelve-color version, or 300 grams of the same yarn for six-color version

Preparing the materials:
Each skein of yarn will weigh 50 grams, and you will need twelve skeins for the twelve-color version, or six for the six-color version. See the explanation in the box on page 56 for an easy way to determine the size of each skein if you do not have a gram scale. Wind the yarn into skeins using your cardboard template, tie the ends of each skein together, and place several loose holding ties around each skein. Wash your yarn in warm water and wet out for 30 minutes or longer while you prepare the dyepots.

Preparing the dyepots:
Mix a stock solution for each of your three primary dye colors, using 1 tsp dye for each 100 ml water. (See instructions on page 22.) You will need a total of 300 ml of yellow, and 200 ml each of red and blue. (More yellow is required to compensate for the relative weakness of yellow dye.)

Place 1500 ml (1½ liters) of hot water in each dyepot. Add 5 tsp salt to each pot and stir well. Now measure dye into the pots according to the following recipe; use measuring cups for large amounts (more than 20 ml), and the 10-ml syringes for small amounts. (See page 29 for instructions on using syringes.) If you have chosen the six-step dye run, use only the odd-numbered steps.

Dyepot	Red	Yellow	Blue
1	50 ml	——	——
(red dyepot)			
2	30 ml	20 ml	——
3	10 ml	40 ml	——
4	2 ml	48 ml	——
5	——	50 ml	——
(yellow dyepot)			
6	——	45 ml	5 ml
7	——	30 ml	20 ml
8	——	15 ml	35 ml
9	——	——	50 ml
(blue dyepot)			
10	10 ml	——	40 ml
11	25 ml	——	25 ml
12	40 ml	——	10 ml

The dye run:
It is helpful to prepare a dye record sheet, like the one on page 25, for each dyepot. It will help you keep track of the progress of each dyepot.

Add one skein of wet cotton to each dyebath. Stir frequently for 15 minutes. Be sure to lift and rotate the skeins to distribute the dye evenly.

Add the fixer at the 15-minute mark. For each dyepot mix 2 tsp sodium carbonate into approximately 50 ml hot water, and stir to dissolve. Working with one dyepot at a time, remove the skein, add the fixer solution, mix well, and return the skein to the dyebath. Repeat until fixer has been added to all the dyepots. Continue to stir dyebaths frequently for the next 15 minutes, then stir occasionally for another 30 minutes.

Pour off and discard the dye. Rinse each skein thoroughly, until the rinse water runs clear. Then wash the skeins, rinse them again, and hang them to dry. Be sure to line them up in color sequence, so you can best enjoy the results of your efforts!

Making the knit baby blankets
Materials required: For two blankets, each approximately 33" × 45", use twelve 50-gram skeins, one each of twelve colors; or, for one blanket, use six 50-gram skeins, one each of six colors. A circular needle 29" or 36" long, size 6 or size required to obtain correct gauge.
Gauge: Approximately 22 stitches = 4" and 30 rows = 4".
Knitting instructions:

Use your colors in order, starting with any one you like. You might work all twelve colors to the center of the blanket, and then work out again to the first color. We chose to knit the blanket from red through to

Project 3: Color Wheel Baby Blankets. *Dye twelve basic colors to make a baby blanket in either weaving or knitting.*

purple, and repeated this sequence twice. Each stripe in our version contained twelve rows, or four repeats of the three-row pattern.

With your first color, cast on 172 stitches. Working back and forth on the needle (do not join into a tube), repeat three rows of pattern: **Row 1:** K1, *K2 tog, K6, yo, K1, yo, K6, K2 tog*, repeat between *s across, end K1. If you put stitch markers between repeats, or sets of two repeats, you'll have help keeping your place in the pattern. **Row 2:** Purl across. **Row 3:** Knit across.

Repeat these three rows throughout, maintaining the consistent color rotation of your choice. Cast off loosely. Sew in ends.

Making the woven baby blankets
Materials and equipment required:
You will need a 36" loom with two or four harnesses. Use twelve 50-gram skeins, in twelve colors, for two blankets approximately 33" × 43" plus 2" fringe on each end, or six 50-gram skeins, in six colors, for one blanket.
Warp length: 3 3/4 yards for two blankets; 2 yards for one blanket
Ends per inch: 10
Width of warp: 33 1/2"
Total warp ends: 336; wind 28 ends of each color for twelve-color version, or 56 ends of each color for six-color version
Threading: We threaded to a twill, or straight draw (1-2-3-4), on a four-harness loom. If you have a two-harness loom, thread for plain weave (1-2-1-2).
Weaving: Use the remainder of your twelve (or six) colors as weft, arranging the colors as you like. We wove the obvious color-gamp sequence, using each of our colors in the order it appeared in the warp. We wove 36 picks (about 3 3/4 ") of each color. Use a light hand on your beater, and try to get just 10 picks per inch, for a balanced weave. You can treadle a twill or plain weave, depending on your equipment and your preference. It might be interesting to try a 3/1 twill, which would be warp-faced on one side and weft-faced on the other. Leave 8" for fringe between blankets (4" will be used on each).

6

Color Mixing

An infinite array of colors is within your reach when you dye your own materials. You can create any color from a small set of starting colors, just by varying the color characteristics of hue, value, and intensity.

The basic colors to start with are the primaries: red, yellow, and blue, plus black for *toning* or lowering the intensity of these hues. It is worth noting that there is not just one obvious set of primary colors with which to begin. Most dye manufacturers offer several reds, blues, and yellows in their basic range of colors. You will have to experiment to find the combination of primaries that yields your preferred color range. For example, a primary set consisting of magenta, turquoise, and lemon yellow (often referred to as "printers' primaries") yields a much brighter overall range of mixed colors than does the more traditional set of red, sky blue, and gold-yellow.

With a little practice, you can become a master at creating a range of *color gradations*, that is, a group of closely related colors which step gradually from one point on the color sphere to another, producing a smooth visual progression. Careful measuring of dye solutions can easily yield a panorama of graded colors.

Value gradations

The simplest place to start is with a series of values of a given color, or a *one-color* value gradation. The four shades of blue we dyed in Project 1, and the eight values of black dyed for the vest in Project 2, are examples of one-color value gradations. It is useful to make a value gradation for every basic color of the dyestuff you are using, so you will have a visual reference of how much dye is required for a light, medium, or dark value of each color. Dye powders are not all exactly the same strength from one color to another. In a given dye system, a value gradation for the basic blue might differ from the identically measured value gradation for the basic red. In general, yellow is the weakest basic shade, red is the strongest, and blue is somewhere between red and yellow in strength.

The way to create a smooth visual progression from a light value of a color to a dark value of that color is to start with a very small amount of dye for the lightest value, and to proceed by doubling the amount of dye in each step until a dark color is achieved. You may have noticed that the four-step dye run for Project 1 was a value progression of this type. An analysis of the dilution system used for that dye run shows that each dyepot contained exactly half as much dye as the preceding pot. In Project 2, we used a more exactly measured

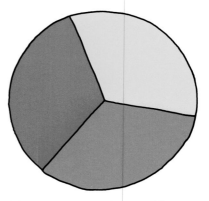

Magenta, turquoise, and lemon yellow, the "printer's primaries," will produce a brighter overall range of mixed colors.

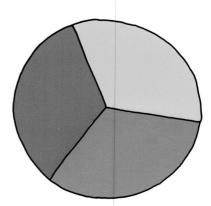

The traditional primaries of red, sky blue, and gold-yellow will result in more conventional mixed colors.

gradation to get the eight value gradations of black. The more precise measuring equipment described in Chapter 3 was used to obtain small changes from one color value to the next.

In Project 2 we put 50 grams of fabric in each dyepot and used the following amounts of dye:

ONE-COLOR GRADATION DYE RUN

light

Pot 1	value 1:	1.25 ml dyestuff
Pot 2	value 2:	2.5 ml dyestuff
Pot 3	value 3:	5 ml dyestuff
Pot 4	value 4:	10 ml dyestuff
Pot 5	value 5:	20 ml dyestuff
Pot 6	value 6:	40 ml dyestuff
Pot 7	value 7:	80 ml dyestuff
Pot 8	value 8:	160 ml dyestuff

dark

The amounts of stock solution in this dye run increase by a *multiple* of two, rather than an addition of two, between steps. This is the first important fact in dye mixing: **Fact 1—A smooth visual progression between colors is achieved with a geometric progression of amounts of dye.** A geometric progression is a series of numbers derived by multiplying each step in the progression by a given amount (in this case, the number 2) to arrive at the next number in the progression. In the example of the value gradation above, the first value, 1.25 ml, is multiplied by 2 to get the second value of 2.5 ml. This value is multiplied by 2 to get the third value of 5 ml, and so on.

The difference in dye amounts between two light values is very small, whereas the difference in dye amounts between two dark values is quite large. This means that pale colors are much more sensitive to dye amount changes than are dark colors. This is the second important fact in color mixing with dyes: **Fact 2—The darker a color, the larger the change in dye amount required to produce a visual change.**

Hue gradations

The practice obtained from creating these value gradations will also help you understand how to create hue, or *two-color*, gradations. Two-color gradations can be used to create a gradual visual progression from one hue to another along the rim of the color wheel. The cotton color-wheel baby blankets in Project 3 illustrate this type of progression. Another two-color gradation, shown in Project 4, goes from one hue to another across the color wheel and creates a range of colors extending from pure hues through dull colors, and back to pure hues again.

Practice at creating a range of colors between any two given colors will give you the confidence and the expertise to zero in on any particular color you need. Suppose, for example, that you want to make a pillow to match your Aunt Bea's couch, which happens to be an unusual shade of burgundy. It is obvious that you will need some red, and a little blue. The task is to narrow down the definition of "some" red and "a little" blue to specific measures of dye. First, you decide if the color is predominantly red or blue. Supposing that it is more red, you start with some red, and add different amounts of blue, creating a range of different burgundies from which to choose. An example of such a two-color gradation follows. We used 10 grams of yarn in each pot for these two sample dye runs.

TWO-COLOR DYE RUN #1

amount of red dye		amount of blue dye
10 ml red	*Pot 1*	0.5 ml blue
10 ml red	*Pot 2*	1 ml blue
10 ml red	*Pot 3*	2 ml blue
10 ml red	*Pot 4*	4 ml blue

Note that you gradually increase the value of your burgundy color as you add more and more blue. If the amount of blue required is small, or if the exact value of the desired shade is not important, this is a satisfactory way to proceed.

There is another way of approaching the same problem to avoid changing the value of the colors you are creating. You hold the total amount of dye constant by decreasing the amount of red as you increase the amount of blue:

TWO-COLOR DYE RUN #2

amount of red dye		amount of blue dye
9.5 ml red	*Pot 1*	0.5 ml blue
9 ml red	*Pot 2*	1 ml blue
8 ml red	*Pot 3*	2 ml blue
6 ml red	*Pot 4*	4 ml blue

Both of these two-color gradations take into account Fact 2, that small changes are adequate at the pale or sensitive end of a gradation, whereas larger steps are required at the dark end. In two-color gradations the sensitive sections of the gradation are at both ends of the gradation; that is, closest to the pure hue ends of the gradation. Our example above focuses on the red end. The blue end is not approached since the burgundy shade desired is toward the red end of this gradation. To obtain the blue end of the gradation, continue as follows:

TWO-COLOR DYE RUN #2 (continued)

amount of red dye		amount of blue dye
4 ml red	*Pot 5*	6 ml blue
2 ml red	*Pot 6*	8 ml blue
1 ml red	*Pot 7*	9 ml blue
0.5 ml red	*Pot 8*	9.5 ml blue

These dye runs yield a range of colors between the two starting-point colors of red and blue. You can invent similar gradations to create a smooth progression of colors along any pathway on the color sphere. Our value-gradation dye run in Project 2 followed a vertical path through the center of the color sphere as it progressed through several values of black. Our two-color gradation produced a range of intense hues between red and blue along the equator of the color sphere.

The following two-color gradation pursues a pathway across the color sphere from one color to its complement. This gradation passes through the muted colors at the center of the color sphere. We used 20-gram skeins of wool in each dyepot.

TWO-COLOR DYE RUN #3:
COMPLEMENTARY COLORS

amount of purple dye		amount of yellow dye
10 ml purple	*Pot 1*	0 ml yellow
9.5 ml purple	*Pot 2*	0.5 ml yellow
9 ml purple	*Pot 3*	1 ml yellow
8 ml purple	*Pot 4*	2 ml yellow
6 ml purple	*Pot 5*	4 ml yellow
4 ml purple	*Pot 6*	6 ml yellow
2 ml purple	*Pot 7*	8 ml yellow
1 ml purple	*Pot 8*	9 ml yellow
0.5 ml purple	*Pot 9*	9.5 ml yellow
0 ml purple	*Pot 10*	10 ml yellow

We enjoyed the results of this unusual color progression so much that we created Project 4 using two versions of this gradation: the purple/yellow version above and a turquoise/orange version. We must confess, however, that we modified the dye runs to make them into smooth visual progressions. See the introduction to Project 4, which follows, for details on these adjustments.

When we had to adapt our theoretical dye run in response to the actual results, we encountered the third important fact of color mixing: **Fact 3—Each color of dye has its own intrinsic value, which determines its ability to influence other dye colors.** If you want the gradations from one color to another to have equal *visual* steps, you must occasionally adjust your dye amounts to fit this somewhat awkward fact. In general, as we have mentioned, yellow has the weakest value, blue has a middle value, and red has the strongest value. This means that it takes less blue to change yellow than it takes yellow to change blue. Similarly, it takes less red to effect a change in either blue or yellow. In fact, red is so much stronger than yellow that it requires only a very small amount of red to affect yellow, and a substantial quantity of yellow to affect red. The secondary and tertiary colors have strengths between those of their neighboring primaries.

As illustrated in these examples, the possibilities of exploration of pathways of color on the color sphere are endless. The information gained from these explorations can be applied to the creation of color gradations or to the search for a single color for a particular purpose. Purposeful exploration of color progressions, together with adequate recordkeeping, will provide you with an encyclopedia of color samples from which to choose.

Project 4: Across-the-Color-Wheel Scarves

designed, dyed, and knit by Betsy Blumenthal

We originally intended that Gradation Dye Run 3 in this chapter would simply illustrate a progression from one hue (purple) to its complement (yellow). Then we fell in love with the progression, and decided to do it again with enough yarn to make a scarf. Curious to see the results of a different "walk across the color wheel," we did a second dye run with two other complements (turquoise and orange) and made a second scarf.

In order to accommodate the large skeins and to adjust for the relative weakness of the yellow and orange dyes, we used different amounts of dye in each pot than were used for Dye Run 3. First, because there was twice as much fiber in each pot we doubled the amount of dye per pot.

Then, for the purple-to-yellow scarf, we compensated for the weakness of the yellow dye by eliminating two steps at the purple end of the run and adding a step at the yellow end. The original dye run had ten steps; our adaptation has nine.

We made different changes in the turquoise-to-orange run. To compensate for the relative weakness of the orange dye, we doubled the amount of orange used throughout the dye run. We also eliminated the all-orange color because it was too bright, and added a few drops of orange to the all-turquoise dyebath to tone it down. The final sequence in this case also has nine steps.

Our goal was to get a series of colors which appears uniformly graded. If you choose other complementary pairs for your dye run, use one of these two adjustment systems, imagining the weaker of your two colors to be in the position of our yellow or orange, and the stronger to be like our purple or turquoise.

Equipment you will need:

- a stove with four burners
- three metal dyepots
- nine wide-mouth canning jars or peanut-butter jars, capacity 4 cups each, for double-boiler dye method
- two measuring cups with metric divisions, capacity at least 250 ml
- two 10-ml syringes
- stir sticks
- cardboard for winding skeins, 18″ × 6″

Materials you will need:

- 200 grams of 100% wool, knitting-worsted weight
- two colors of fiber-reactive dye, at least 1 tbsp (approx. 15 gm) of each; we used Violet 81 and Yellow 14 Cibacron, from Pro-Chem, for the first scarf, and Turquoise 40 and Orange 22 Cibacron, from Pro-Chem, for the second scarf
- ½ cup (¼ pound) salt
- 1 cup (240 ml) 5% acetic acid (white vinegar), used as the fixer for fiber-reactive dye on wool

Preparing the materials:

You will need nine 20-gram skeins, one for each color in the gradation. Wind the skeins and tie them; see the shortcut instructions for winding a set of small equal skeins on page 56. Wash the skeins in warm water and mild detergent,
rinse several times, and leave to wet out while you prepare the dye and dyebaths.

Preparing the dye:

You will need 150 ml of yellow dye and 100 ml of violet dye for the first scarf, or 150 ml of turquoise and 250 ml of orange for the second scarf. Mix stock solutions according to the directions on page 22, using 1 tsp of dye for every 100 ml of water.

Preparing the dyepots:

In order to spend just one dye-run's amount of time at the stove, we contrived a "double-boiler" method which lets us process all nine colors at once. We use one of the canning jars for each of the colors, arranging three jars in each metal dyepot. We use enough water in the metal pot to keep the jars from cracking through direct exposure to heat. In order to keep the dyebaths as hot as possible, we cover the pots except when we're stirring them.

To get ready, line up the nine dye-pot jars and prepare them as follows:

1. Place 600 ml (about ⅔ quart) of water in each jar.

2. Add 1 tsp salt to each jar.

3. Add dye to each jar, using one of the recipe sequences listed below. (See page 29 on measuring with syringes.)

Dyes

Pot	Violet	Yellow	Turq.	Orange
1	20 ml	0 ml	20 ml	drop
2	18 ml	2 ml	19 ml	2 ml
3	12 ml	8 ml	18 ml	4 ml
4	8 ml	12 ml	16 ml	8 ml
5	4 ml	16 ml	12 ml	16 ml
6	2 ml	18 ml	8 ml	24 ml
7	1 ml	19 ml	4 ml	32 ml
8	0.5 ml	19.5 ml	2 ml	36 ml
9	0 ml	20 ml	1 ml	38 ml

The dye run:

Put three jars in each of the three metal pots, surround the jars with several inches of water, and place the pots on the stove. Turn on the heat. Stir the dye in each jar carefully, then add one skein of wetted wool and mix again. Continue to stir all nine pots gently, and heat them to a simmer.

At the 15-minute mark, add fixer. Working with one dye jar at a time, remove the skein, add 20 ml of white vinegar to the jar, mix well, return the skein, and stir gently. Repeat until there is fixer in all nine jars.

Continue to stir frequently but gently for 15 minutes. The water around the jars should be boiling, and the liquid in the jars should be steaming hot or simmering. Continue to simmer the dyepots for another 30 minutes, stirring occasionally. You can cover the dyepots during this period.

Project 4: *Across-the-Color-Wheel Scarves.* *Dye a progression of colors from one color to its complement to get fascinating muted hues. Then knit them into a winter scarf.*

At the end of the one-hour dye run, turn off the heat and allow the jars to cool until they're just warm. They will cool faster if you take them out of the metal pots. When the dye liquid is at room temperature, rinse each skein thoroughly in warm water. Then combine the skeins and wash and rinse gently, keeping the water at an even warm temperature. Hang to dry.

Knitting the scarf:

Wind your yarn from the skeins into balls. Begin with a color from one end of your color gradation.

With size 8 needles, cast on 40 stitches. Work in K1, P1 rib for 5″. Without breaking off the first yarn, change to the next color and knit four rows (about 1″). Now, without breaking either yarn, return to the first color and knit four rows (about 1″). To make a neat edge when you are carrying the resting yarn through the 1″ stripes, wrap the working yarn around the resting yarn as you begin rows at the edge where the yarn is being carried.

After working the second 1″ stripe, break off the first color and knit 5″ with the second color. Start the third color as you began the second, with a 1″ stripe of color 3, a 1″ stripe of color 2, and continuing with color 3.

Repeat this stripe pattern, with wide stripes and narrow stripes alternating, throughout. End with 5″ of color 9.

Darn in loose ends of yarn. Use extra yarn to make tassels and sew them on the edge, arranging the colors as you choose.

Small amounts of yarn can be dyed by the double-boiler method, where jars of different dyes are heated in the same pot.

EQUAL WEIGHT SKEINS WITHOUT A SCALE

If you do not have a gram scale, you can use this easy method to **subdivide large skeins or cones** of yarn into any required number of equal-sized smaller skeins. You will need to know how many yards are in your larger package of yarn, and how much the skein or cone weighs. The method works by measuring the yards, rather than weight, in each skein.

For example, for Project 4 we need nine equal-sized skeins of wool, each weighing 20 grams. Since there are about 200 yards in a 100-gram skein of knitting-worsted wool, we will use this figure in our explanation.

Step 1: Calculate the yardage in one 20-gram skein. Since there are 200 yards in 100 grams, and 20 grams = $\frac{1}{5}$ of 100 grams, a 20-gram skein will contain $\frac{1}{5}$ of 200 yards, or 40 yards.

Step 2: Using a piece of cardboard 18″ long, wind forty rounds to obtain a 40-yard skein. Tie the ends together, and tie several loose ties around the skein, using a few extra feet of yarn. Repeat until all nine skeins have been wound:

Project 5: Woven Silk Scarf

designed, dyed, and woven by Betsy Blumenthal

This project introduces the pre-metallized dyes, which can be used on all protein fibers (wool, silk, alpaca, and so forth). They are slightly more complicated to use than the union and fiber-reactive dyes in Projects 1 through 4. They require two more chemical assistants, as well as heat—you'll need metal dyepots and a stove. Pre-metallized dyes produce rich colors with a minimum amount of dye, so they are very economical if you frequently need to obtain strong colors on wool or silk.

You can substitute either fiber-reactive or acid dyes for this project, although they will produce somewhat paler colors. See pages 39–40 for the methods of using these dyes.

The dye runs for this project introduce three-color dye recipes; so far, you've only used two-color mixes. A mix of three hues in one pot generally produces a more muted blend than a two-color combination. The third color we use in each pot here is the complement of the mix of the other two colors. Used in small amounts, it tones, or lowers the brilliance of, the finished color. We use only very small amounts of this third color, so we don't mute the basic color much. If you would like your colors to be toned down more, use more of the third color in each of the recipes below. If you would like darker and more brilliant colors than ours, double all dye amounts in each pot.

Equipment you will need:

- four enamel or stainless-steel dyepots, to hold at least 1 gallon each
- four measuring cups with metric divisions, capacity at least 250 ml
- four bottles, or extra cups, for dye stock solutions
- plastic measuring spoons
- four 10-ml syringes
- dishwashing gloves
- stir sticks
- cardboard to wind skeins, 18″ × 6″
- pH paper, sensitive in the range 4.0 to 7.0 (available at most drug stores)

Materials you will need (see appendix for sources):

- 250 grams natural silk yarn, with about 100 yards/ounce
- 50 grams natural bouclé silk yarn, with about 60 yards/ounce
- one small package (½ ounce) each of pre-metallized dye (we used Telana, or Lanaset), in each of four colors: Turquoise, Royal Blue, Yellow, and Scarlet
- 2 cups 5% acetic acid (white vinegar)
- small package (1 ounce) Glauber's salt
- small container (1 ounce) Albegel Set
- (1 ounce) sodium acetate

Preparing the materials:

You will need four skeins: two 50-gram skeins plus one 150-gram skein of the natural silk yarn, and one 50-gram skein of the natural silk bouclé. (See page 56 for an easy measuring method.) Wash all the skeins in warm water, rinse them, and leave them to wet out while you prepare the dyes and the dyebaths.

Preparing the dye:

You will need 50 ml of stock solution each for Yellow, Scarlet, and Blue, and 200 ml of stock solution for Turquoise. Use ¼ tsp of dye to each 50 ml of water when you mix the stock solutions. (See details for pre-metallized dyes on page 41, and mixing information on page 22.)

Preparing the dyepots:

Place 3 liters (3000 ml) of hot water in one pot, and 1 liter (1000 ml) of hot water into each of the other three pots. Be sure to keep the pot with more water separate, since it will hold the 150-gram skein and will need more of each of the chemicals. Add chemicals to the dyepots as follows:

	for 50 gm *(1 l water)*	for 150 gm *(3 l water)*
5% acetic acid (white vinegar)	20 ml	60 ml
Glauber's salt	1 tsp	3 tsp
sodium acetate	½ tsp	1½ tsp
Albegel Set	0.5 ml	1.5 ml

Stir the dyepots well. Use the pH paper to see that the solution registers between 4.5 and 5.0. If the solution is too acid (below 4.5), add small amounts of sodium acetate; if it is too basic (above 5.0), add small amounts of acetic acid. Check again.

Add the wet fiber to each pot, being sure that the 150-gram skein is in the appropriate pot. Allow to stand for 10 minutes. While the yarn soaks, prepare the dye for each pot using a measuring cup to store each color. Use the following dye recipes:

Color A (on 50 grams of silk)
    30 ml Turquoise
    20 ml Yellow
    2 ml Scarlet

Color B (on 50 grams of silk)
    40 ml Blue
    10 ml Turquoise
    2 ml Scarlet

Color C (on 150 grams of silk)
    150 ml Turquoise

Color D (on 50 grams of bouclé)
    45 ml Scarlet
    5 ml Yellow
    2 ml Turquoise

The dye run:

Place the dyepots with the pre-soaked yarn on the stove and turn heat to low. Working with one pot at a time, remove the yarn, add the appropriate dye solution, stir well, and replace the yarn. Stir thoroughly before you proceed to the next pot.

Continuing to stir frequently, *gradually* raise the temperature to steaming (about 190°F) over a period of 30–45 minutes. Hold the dyepot at this temperature for another 20–30 minutes, or until the dyebath is exhausted (that is, until all the dye is in the fiber and the water is clear).

Project 5: Woven Silk Scarf. *Pre-metallized dyes produce rich colors on silk. These instructions produce enough yarn for two scarves—one for yourself and one for a gift.*

Remove the dyepots from the heat and allow them to cool for an hour or more (overnight is fine). When the liquid is at room temperature, rinse the yarn well and hang it to dry.

Weaving the scarves:

You will need a four-harness loom for this project, although it can be narrow. If you have only a two-harness loom, follow our directions but use plain weave instead of point twill.

The materials are just enough for a 5-yard warp, which will make two scarves, 64″ long plus 4″ fringe. To prepare the yarns for warping, wind each skein into a ball. Make your warp according to the specifications and color plan below. Note that you will wind an extra end of bouclé at each side; this will be used as a floating selvedge. You will have almost half of each color of yarn left, to use as weft.

Warp length: 5 yards

Ends per inch: 12 (to accommodate the bouclé, we used an 8-dent reed and threaded single/double across, to produce 12 e.p.i.)

Width in reed: 10″

Total warp ends: 120

Yarn key: A = silk, B = silk, C = silk, D = bouclé.

Color plan: 1D (floating), *1D, 12C, 1D, 12A, 1D, 12C, 1D, 12B*, repeat once, end 1D, 12C, 1D, 1D (floating).

Threading: Align the point twill threading so the point falls on the bouclé (color D, boldface on draft), using the bouclé also for the floating selvedge on each side:

Weaving: Weave in point twill treadling, reproducing the color order of the warp in the weft. Change the direction of the twill line at each bouclé thread, as in the warp. To catch the floating selvedge with each pick, establish a habit of putting your shuttle into the shed *over* the floating selvedge, and taking it out of the shed *under* the selvedge thread. Use as many repeats as you need to weave the 64″ length. Leave 10″ unwoven between the two scarves, to be used as fringe. After removing the fabric from the loom, trim fringes even and tie overhand knots to secure the warp ends, using four or five ends per knot.

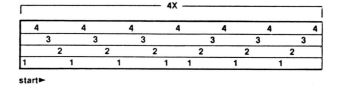

start▶

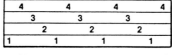

cont.▶   end

7

Other Application Techniques

When you are learning a new craft, it is important to master the correct methods for all the techniques involved. *Then* you can vary the rules to suit your unique purposes. Before you change the rules, it is important to know what parts of the technique are necessary and what parts can be varied. In dyeing, the most changeable ingredient is the method of applying the dye to the fiber. The amount of dye required for a certain value remains the same, the chemicals required to fix the dye remain the same (with some minor variations), but the application method can be varied in a number of exciting ways.

Now that you have mastered the basics of controlled dyeing, you are ready to pursue some of these creative byways. So far, you've explored immersion dyeing. In this chapter we will discuss several alternate application techniques, and provide projects to illustrate them. We strongly recommend that you experiment with these techniques and make samples before you attempt large projects. The unpredictability of these techniques is what makes them so exciting. That same quality can also cause complete disasters. If you make samples, you will know what works best.

We should say at the outset that this discussion is only an introduction to the possibilities. We hope that you will venture further than the scope of our presentation, and we have provided a list of references in the appendix.

Dip-dyeing

Perhaps the easiest of these alternate techniques is dip- or space-dyeing. This technique produces yarns or fabrics dyed in more than one color. For example, a space-dyed yarn might be yellow for twelve inches, blue for twelve inches, and green for twelve inches, then repeat yellow, blue, green for its entire length. A space-dyed fabric might be dark blue at one end and purple at the other, with a range of middle hues in between. Space-dyeing is a variant of immersion dyeing. It is also called dip-dyeing because the different colors are often achieved by dipping first one section of the fiber in a dyepot and then dipping another section into another dyepot.

There are several ways to dip-dye your material. One way is to suspend part of your fiber above the first dyepot, dyeing only half of the skein. After this first dye run is complete and the fiber has been washed, the skein is hung in reverse and another color is applied to the other half. A third color, which is a blend of the first and second colors, is created at the borderline between the two colors.

GENERAL PROCEDURES FOR DIP-DYEING

1. Follow the immersion dye recipe appropriate to the dye-stuff and fiber being used.

2. Calculate the weight of the material based on the amount of fiber actually being immersed in each pot. For example, if you are withholding half of a 100-gram skein from the dyepot, the weight of material actually in the pot will be 50 grams.

3. Take care to avoid dripping dyes in your work area. Since the skein being dyed is pre-wetted, it will drip onto your work surface if you simply drape it over the edge of the pot. The dye will gradually follow the water, and will wick along the fiber onto the work surface. You should contrive a way to suspend your skeins over the dyepot or plan to dye both colors simultaneously with two dyepots placed close together.

4. There is no reason to limit yourself to two dyed sections on a given skein or piece of material. It is easy to devise ways of rotating your fiber into three or more dyepots. Anything goes; let your imagination be your guide and create your own designer yarns and fabrics.

Resist techniques

A glance at the previous section shows that the effects achieved through the random application of dyes are exciting and unique. In many cultures different ways to apply dyes unevenly have been developed and refined into art forms. These techniques are collectively referred to as *resist techniques*, since each depends on some form of withholding sections of the fiber from the dye. The fold-dye technique sampled in Project 8 is an example of one of these methods. In this case the tight folds in the fabric prevent the dye from reaching the fabric inside the folded area.

There are three basic categories of textile resist techniques:
   1. **Tie resists** on fabric
   2. **Paste or wax resists** on fabric
   3. **Bound resists** on yarn

All resist techniques require that the fabric or yarn be prepared to resist the dye before it is placed in the dyepot. The fiber is then dyed with regular immersion dyeing techniques. In multicolor resist textiles, the complexity of the design depends on the skillful use of the resist technique and the application of several colors of dye in successive dye runs, with the resist areas being changed between dye runs.

We will introduce and illustrate these techniques in the following section. We intend only to whet your appetite. The list of resources in the appendix will lead you to a variety of books on these skills of the dyer's art.

Tie resists

This category of resists includes *fold resists* (since these are often tied to prevent the fabric from unfolding), simple *gather-and-bind techniques*, and the more complex *stitched-and-gathered tie resists*. All of these techniques are used on fabric that has already been woven. The fabric is dyed in an immersion dyebath. The operating principle is that the dye is unable to penetrate the areas of the fabric that are tightly folded or bound. The material used to bind the fabric is chosen for its ability to resist the dye being used. Popular tying materials are rubber bands or strips of plastic bags, as these will resist any dyestuff. Cotton cord or a tightly twisted linen will also create a resist.

The shape of the resist section depends on the type of folding or gathering used and the placement of the ties. It is very important to make the ties tight. Even the most apparently carefree patterns are usually well planned. The fabric is changed from a flat sheet into an organized clump. For a crazed crystalline effect, the fabric is crushed into a wad and wrapped tightly. For horizontal and/or vertical lines the fabric is accordion-pleated and bound at intervals. Circles are made by gathering the fabric at a point and binding.

To try a stitch resist using a sewing machine, sketch the lines which you want to have resist the dye with tailor's chalk. Fold the fabric on one of these lines, and stitch close to the fold. Repeat until all the lines have been stitched.

Wax or paste resists

In these resists, a liquid is applied to the fabric surface; the liquid hardens after it has been applied and resists the dye. After the fabric is dyed, the resist material is removed, leaving undyed areas on a dyed background. The process is repeated with successive applications of the resist material and additional dye runs, for complex multicolored patterns. The most well-known of these resists is *batik*, which originated in Indonesia and India. In most batik resists, a mixture of paraffin and beeswax is the resist material. The wax is applied hot and solidifies as it cools. Special pen-like tools for holding the wax, called *tjantings,* are used to apply the dye in a freehand manner. An alternate method of applying the wax is with a stamping tool, or *tjap*, made of iron on wood. The tjap is dipped in the wax and then stamped onto the fabric, each stamp carefully aligned with the previous stamp to form a repeat pattern. Other resist materials, primarily a variety of starch pastes made from plants such as rice or cassava, are used in traditional resist fabrics throughout the Far East and Africa. In Japan and China, the rice-paste resist is often applied over a cut stencil so that the resist adheres only in the cut-out area. As with the stamped-wax resists of Indonesia, the stencils are used repeatedly in careful patterns to form an overall design on the fabric.

A synthetic resist material known as *gutta* has been developed recently. Gutta behaves like a wax resist but does not require heat. The gutta itself can contain dye, so that the line which is left when the gutta is removed from the fabric can itself be colored.

Bound resists

This is the resist treatment in which the yarns to be woven (either the warp or the weft or both) are dyed before being woven, knitted, crocheted, or otherwise worked. This process is often called *ikat*, its Indonesian name. Ikat resist techniques can be used to create wonderfully intricate patterning with characteristic feathered edges due to the slight shifting of the threads during warping and weaving. Traditional ikats are native to the Far East, with elaborate traditions of ikat textiles found in Indonesia, India, Japan, and China. There are also ikat fabrics in the Middle East and throughout Africa and South America. Ikats are categorized by the placement of the resist treatment. Thus there are warp ikats, weft ikats, and compound and double ikats. Compound and double ikats have resist areas in both warp and weft. In compound ikats the warp and weft areas are independent. In double ikats the warp and weft areas are designed to deliberately coincide.

The material used to bind off the yarns before dyeing is chosen for its ability to resist the dyestuff being used. For example, a cotton yarn will not be affected by an acid dye and can be used as a resist material on wool yarn. Other materials—such as rubber bands, strips from plastic bags, and plastic tape—will work on all fiber types and resist all dyes.

Our warp-ikat project introduces this technique. The blue fiber-reactive dye approximates the traditional blue of indigo used by the Japanese for their cotton ikat fabrics.

Ikat is a traditional technique in many cultures. A bound resist, used on the warp or weft yarn before weaving, allows dye to penetrate some sections while leaving others undyed. These ethnic textiles all demonstrate warp ikat.

Rainbow dyeing

Throw caution to the winds and leave your measuring equipment behind! *Rainbow dyeing* is a catch-all term for a method of dyeing in which the dye is dropped, splashed, sprayed, or poured randomly on fabric or yarn to create unevenly dyed multicolor fiber. Most of the rules for immersion dyeing are directed toward an evenly dyed product and therefore do not apply to rainbow dyeing. In rainbow dyeing, the fiber pre-soaks in the fixer before the dye is applied. The procedures you use will vary, depending on the dye and the type of fiber.

GENERAL PROCEDURES FOR RAINBOW DYEING

1. Apply whatever dyestuff you are using in liquid form. If your dye is not purchased as a liquid, mix a stock solution from the powdered dye according to the instructions in Chapter 3. Use fiber-reactive or union dyes for cellulose fiber, and fiber-reactive, acid, or pre-metallized dyes for wool or silk.

2. Follow the same safety precautions as for immersion dyeing.

Stitch-resist and tie-resist techniques are used to produce special dye effects. White fabric, bound and dyed with indigo, is traditional in several cultures.

3. Weigh the materials. Prepare the yarns in fold-type skeins, with several ties, or leave the yarn in balls or pull-type skeins.

4. Wash and wet-out materials.

5. Prepare pre-dye soaking baths with salt and chemical assistants required for the weight of yarn or fabric you plan to dye. (See the dye recipe pages in Chapter 4 for the amounts.) For dark colors double the amounts of salt and fixer. In this method all of the chemicals are added to the pre-soak, whereas in immersion dyeing the chemicals are added over a period of time.

6. Pre-soak the fiber or fabric for 30 to 45 minutes in the pre-soak solution.

7. Remove the fiber from the pre-soak, and wring out excess moisture.

8. (*For cellulose fibers, skip to step 12.*) **Protein fibers** need to be heated to fix the dyes. Possible methods are:

> A. In a covered casserole dish in an oven at 200 degrees Fahrenheit for 30 minutes.
>
> B. In a covered dish in a microwave for 5 or more minutes at full power.*
>
> C. On the stove in a steamer. Put an inch of water in the bottom of the steamer and simmer covered for 15 minutes.

9. Place the fibers in the pot. Fleece can be packed in tightly. Pour or sprinkle the dye on the fiber. A syringe is good for this and can be used to squeeze dye inside the skeins.

10. Heat the fibers. Be sure the fibers remain damp, especially in the casserole and microwave methods.

11. Allow fibers to cool to room temperature. Wash and rinse. *Protein fibers are finished at this point.*

12. For **cellulose fibers:** lay the yarn or fabric on a large piece of plastic. Apply dyes by spraying, dripping, painting, pouring, etc. The dye does not wick, so places not covered in dye at this point will remain undyed.

---

* The safety of using a microwave oven for both cooking and dyeing is a matter for discussion, not yet resolved.

13. Carefully roll the dyed fiber in the plastic, sealing the ends of the roll. Allow to sit out of direct sunlight for between six and twenty-four hours.

14. Wash and rinse. *Cellulose fibers are finished at this point.*

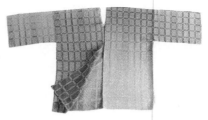

Dyed silk hippari jacket by Betsy Blumenthal

Project 6: Dip-Dye Woven Rug. *By dipping each skein only halfway into the dye, you can make two-color skeins to use as weft for a pair of rugs.*

Project 6: Dip-Dye Woven Rug

designed, dyed, and woven by Betsy Blumenthal

Dip-dyeing is an easy way to obtain multicolor yarns or fabrics. We used the technique to apply color to one portion of some wool yarn which we used for weft in a rug. When we wove the rug, we lined up the dyed portions on one side and kept the other side in the original neutral colors of our yarn. Since the dyed portion didn't align perfectly, the center section of the rug contained both dyed and neutral yarn and produced an interesting blended effect.

Dip-dyeing requires some advance planning and a system for holding skeins of yarn above the dyepot, so the undyed section stays clear. Otherwise it is no more difficult than a regular dye run.

We decided to make our finished rug 28" wide, and used this dimension to determine what size would produce a weft yarn where the dyed portion would lie along one side when we wove the rug. For this width, we would need at least 28" for each weft pick, plus an allowance for shrinkage and take-up; we planned on 32" of wool for each pick. Our skeins would need to be 64" around, or equal to two weft picks.

We wound skeins in three different neutral colors, and put a skein of each type into every dyepot so there would be variety in the "background," or neutral, part of our rug. We ran six dyepots, producing three warm and three cool overdyed tones. The differences in the original colors show up only slightly in the overdyed areas. If you prefer, you can use one neutral color for your weft, and wind skeins containing three times as much yardage. Our six colors of wool gave us enough weft for two rugs. We wove one rug using mostly the three cool colors, and the other using mostly the three warm colors.

Equipment you will need:

- three enamel or stainless-steel dyepots, to hold at least 2 gallons each.
- three measuring cups with metric divisions, capacity at least 250 ml
- three bottles or extra measuring cups, for dye stock solutions, capacity at least 400 ml
- plastic measuring spoons
- three 10-ml syringes
- dishwashing gloves
- stir sticks
- cardboard to wind skeins, 32" long, or a skein winder which can be set for a 64" circumference
- arrangement for suspending skeins above dyepot: We used two dowels suspended horizontally about 24" above the stove, and then tied our skeins to the dowels. If this type of set-up is not possible, you can simply drape the skeins over the edge of the pot—as long as you are very careful that the wool is kept away from the burners.

Materials you will need:

- about 600 grams (1½ pounds) *each* of three pale neutral gray or tan shades of rug wool, at between 720 and 800 yards/pound; or 1800 grams (4½ pounds) of one color
- one package (1 ounce) each of acid dye in Yellow, Red, and Blue
- 1 cup (½ pound) salt

- 1 quart 5% acetic acid (white vinegar)
- 500 grams (about 1¼ pounds, or 650 yards) of 8/4 linen or 4/4 cotton rug warp, or double strands of 8/4 cotton, for rug warp

Preparing the materials:

You will need eighteen skeins, six each of the three neutral colors. Using a circumference of 64" for each skein, wind 100 rounds per skein. It is easiest to wind the skeins on a swift which can be firmly set to the right size, but a piece of stiff cardboard will suffice for a template. Tie several loose ties and one tight tie on each skein. If your yarn is of the weight we suggest, your skeins will weigh about 100 grams each. If you are using just one background color, wind six skeins with about 300 rounds per skein (these will weigh about 300 grams each).

Cut six 24" cotton cords. Make six bundles of three skeins each, using one skein of each neutral color in each bundle. Slip the cord through the tight tie on each of the three skeins in a bundle and tie tightly, leaving 10" tails. The tails will be used to suspend the bundle of skeins above the dyepot. Wash the skeins, rinse them, and leave them to soak, with only the bottom half of each skein in the wetting-out water.

Preparing the dye:

You will need 350 ml of stock solution of Red, 100 ml of Yellow, and 250 ml of Blue. Use ½ tsp of dye to each 100 ml of water (see also page 22).

Preparing the dyepots:

We calculated the amounts of dyes and chemicals in each dyepot on the basis of 150 grams of fiber. Each bundle of skeins weighs about 300 grams, but only half of every bundle will be in the dyepot so we divided this full amount by two.

The master dye recipe (page 40) gives you detailed information on using acid dyes. It is handy to use a dye record sheet (page 25) to track the progress of each dyepot.

With only four burners on our stove, we used three at a time and dyed the three warm tones first and the three cool tones second. The specifics for the six pots in this dye run are as follows:

1. Place 4500 ml (4.5 liters) water in each pot.

2. Add 1½ tbsp (7½ tsp) salt to each pot.

3. Add dye to each pot as follows, and stir well.

Warm tones:

Pot 1:
50 ml Red, 70 ml Yellow, 1 ml Blue
Pot 2:
80 ml Red, 20 ml Yellow, 3 ml Blue

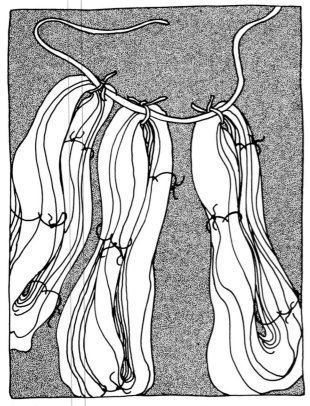

Tie several loose ties and one tight tie on each skein. Make six bundles of three skeins each by slipping cotton cord through the tight ties.

Tie the cotton cord securely, leaving 10" tails. Use the tails of cord to suspend the bundles from a dowel above the dyepots, so that only half of each skein enters the dye.

Pot 3:
80 ml Red, 2 ml Yellow, 20 ml Blue
Cool tones:
Pot 4:
60 ml Red, 2 ml Yellow, 40 ml Blue
Pot 5:
40 ml Red, 2 ml Yellow, 60 ml Blue
Pot 6:
20 ml Red, 2 ml Yellow, 80 ml Blue

Using two yarns as one, arrange the colored area of your weft so that it forms blocks of color.

Place the dyepots on the stove and suspend one bundle of skeins above each pot. Half (16") of each bundle needs to be immersed in the dye solution while half (16") is held above it. Turn the burners to low. Heat the dyepots to a simmer over the next 30 minutes, stirring often.

At the 30-minute mark, add 5% acetic acid (vinegar) to each dyepot. Work with one dyepot at a time. Remove the bundle of yarn, add 75 ml of acetic acid to the pot, stir well, and return the wool to the pot. Stir often for another 15 minutes. Then repeat the addition of acetic acid, as above, for a total of 150 ml of acetic acid per pot.

Simmer for 15 minutes more. Turn off heat and allow the dyebaths to

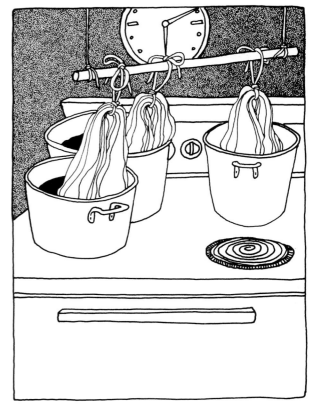

cool to room temperature, with the skeins still half in and half out of the dyepot. Wash and rinse the skeins and hang them to dry. Admire your results.

Weaving the rugs:

You will need a two- or four-harness loom with at least 28" weaving width, and a 6- or 12-dent reed. The dyed wool weft is enough for two closely packed weft-faced rugs, each about 28" × 48". You will need about 650 yards of warp. We used an 8/4 linen, but you can substitute 4/4 cotton or a double strand of 8/4 cotton. (The rug will not be as firm with the cotton as with the linen warp.)

Warp length: 3¾ yards
Ends per inch: 6
Width in reed: 28"
Total warp ends: 170 (168, plus 2 selvedge ends)
Threading: Thread a four-harness loom to a straight draw (1–2–3–4), or a two-harness loom to plain weave. Double the outermost two ends at each side, in both heddle and reed, for a selvedge.
Weaving: Treadle plain weave, alternating 1,3 and 2,4 (four-harness) or 1 and 2 (two-harness) throughout.

Wind all of the skeins into balls. Choose either the warm tones (from dyepots 1, 2, and 3) or the cool tones (dyepots 4, 5, and 6) to be your main color (MC) on your first rug. You can weave each color in any amount you choose, or follow our plan. We used a double strand of wool for weft throughout the rug.

Our weave plan begins with the choice of two of the nine possible shades of MC (or one of the three possible shades of MC if you made only six skeins). Wind a shuttle with both colors held together, being careful to align the dyed and the neutral areas of both strands as you wind.

Weave 3", lining up the dyed half of your weft with the left side of the rug. For each pick, use the angle of your weft to adjust the placement of the yarn and keep the colored portion where you want it on the left side. For maximum blending at the center of the rug, allow the dividing point between dyed and undyed portions to move back and forth as you proceed. Actually, once you've established the correct angle for your weft this variation usually happens by itself. You'll just watch the main

and background colors place themselves, and make small adjustments when you want to.

At the 3" mark, end the first weft. Choose two other MC shades, wind them together on the shuttle, and weave another 3", with the colored portion aligned to the right this time.

After 3", end the second MC weft and weave 1" using two of the alternate colors (AC) stranded together.

Proceed in this manner, with 3" MC, 3" MC, 1" AC, until the rug measures 48". End with 3" MC, 3" MC. Note that since the rug is measured under tension on the loom, the completed rug will be shorter than 48"; our finished rugs measure 46" plus fringe.

Finish your rugs with a knotted edge of your choice, and leave fringe loose or in braids or twists, as desired.

Notes: Depending on the relative sizes and firmness of your warp and weft yarns, you may have difficulty packing the weft yarn in so it completely covers the warp. If this is the case, here are some hints:
• Insert your weft at a generous, bubbled angle; close the shed before you beat, to force your weft to remain evenly distributed.
• Use a tapestry beater or kitchen fork to pack the weft in by hand. After every inch or so of weaving, stop and work across the fell of the rug with a firm pull on the loom's beater.
• Use a loom with a heavy beater, or add weight to your beater (an iron rod works well).
• If all else fails, re-sley your warp at 5 ends per inch, discarding the extra ends.

Alternate warm colors on one side with cool colors on the other side.

Project 7: Stitch-resist Samples and Scarf

designed, stitched, and dyed by Kathryn Kreider

The stitch-resist technique has been developed by traditional artisans throughout the world. It is known by many names: in Nigeria, it is *adire,* in Japan *shibori.* The resist areas are created by tightly binding an area of fabric with sewing so that it will resist the dye. This produces a smaller, finer pattern than the more familiar tie-dye resists, and allows sharp lines, shapes, and figures to be made. Raffia, linen, and silk have often been used for binding threads, because of their strength, ability to resist dye, and availability.

You can use a sewing machine to stitch the resist lines with results similar to those in the traditional textiles. The success of the final product depends on your understanding of your sewing machine's capabilities and limitations. We suggest you familiarize yourself with its potential for this technique by working the samples described here before you start a project.

Equipment you will need:

- sewing machine
- one plastic (or other) dyepot, to hold 2 gallons
- one measuring cup with metric divisions, capacity at least 250 ml
- one bottle with lid, to store stock solution
- dishwashing gloves
- stir stick
- tailor's chalk or washable marker
- ruler or straightedge

Materials you will need:

- 1 yard of fabric, washed, dried, and ironed; we used Spun Viscose Challis from Test Fabrics
- polyester thread, of good quality in any bright color
- small amount of fiber-reactive dye; we used 1 tsp Navy 47 and ½ tsp Turquoise 40 Cibacron, from Pro-Chem
- ¼ cup salt
- 1 ounce (3 tsp) fixer (sodium carbonate)

Sewing the resist samples:

Cut a scarf 14″ wide from the end of the fabric (it will be about 40–45″ long) and set it aside for your project. Cut six 8″ × 8″ pieces from the remaining fabric for samples. Draw the lines or shapes illustrated in the figure on the fabric, using chalk or marker and the ruler. Using a strong, brightly colored polyester thread on your sewing machine, and the largest basting stitch, sew all the lines. Leave

Stitch your design on the fabric. Then pull the threads into very tight gathers and secure the

ends of the stitching threads. Dye the bundle. We tried six different designs for our samples.

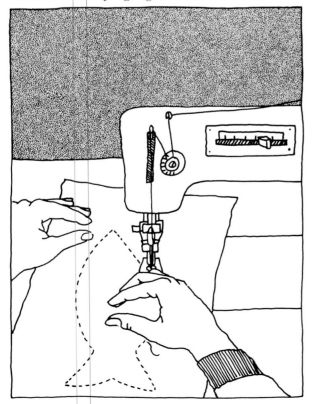

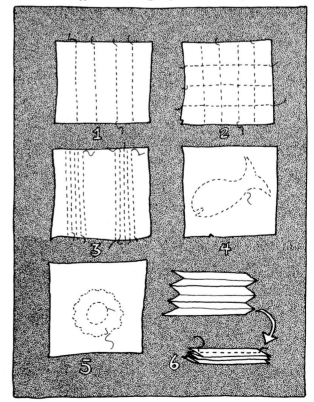

Project 7: Stitch-Resist Samples and Scarf. *Try several stitch-resist patterns on small swatches, then choose your favorite to make a rayon scarf.*

a 3″ tail at the start and end of each row of stitching. When you have completed all the stitching, carefully draw up the fabric along each basting line until the fabric is very tightly packed. (It is easiest to draw up close parallel lines simultaneously.) Knot the ends.

Do *not* wet out the fabric. Smooth dyeing is not important in this technique, and the resist is more effective if the fabric is dry along the stitching lines.

Preparing the dye:

Mix a standard stock solution of fiber-reactive dye, using 1 tsp Navy and ½ tsp Turquoise in 150 ml of water. (See page 22.) This will be enough dye for one set of samples and the project.

Preparing the sample dyebath:

Your six samples together will weigh about 25 grams. Prepare the dyebath with 750 ml hot water, 1 tbsp salt, and 50 ml of the Navy/Turquoise stock solution. Stir well. Place all six dry samples in the dyebath. Stir enough to ensure that each is wet with dye, but do not stir continuously. After 15 minutes, remove cloth, add 1 tsp fixer, and reimmerse cloth. Allow the dyebath to sit for another 30–45 minutes. Pour off the dye, then rinse the fabric thoroughly. Remove the stitching and wash the fabric in warm water with a mild liquid detergent. Rinse until the water runs clear.

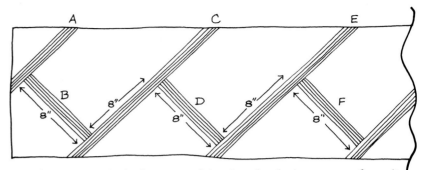

Here's how we stitched our scarf, basing the design on our favorite sample.

Sewing the scarf resist:

Select the best resist pattern from your samples. If none of your patterns has high enough contrast, try several more samples, using a tighter binding.

Design a repeat for your pattern and stitch your scarf according to your design; we chose the third sample as our pattern. Stitch the scarf as follows:

1. Draw the resist lines on the scarf.

2. Sew with a basting stitch along line A, then stitch four more close parallel lines above A, with ¼″ between each pair of lines.

3. Stitch line B and its four parallel lines.

4. Continue in this manner with lines C through G.

5. When all sewing is complete, carefully draw up and tie each set of five parallel threads, proceeding in order from A to G. You should be able to pull each set as a unit.

Dyeing the scarf:

Your scarf weighs about 50 grams. Use the remaining 100 ml of stock solution, 1500 ml water, and 2 tbsp of salt. Follow the dye procedure above, adding 2 tsp of soda at the 15-minute mark.

Rinse thoroughly and remove the stitching. Wash and rinse again. After your scarf has dried you may want to finish the edges by turning a ¼″ hem along each edge.

Project 8: Gutta-resist Scarves

designed by Kathryn Kreider

Painting dyes directly onto silk is a popular technique developed recently in France, from a standard industrial technique used on fashion fabrics. The method combines a resist, similar to the wax resists used in batik textiles, with direct painting of the dyes. The resist is known as Gutta Serti; it has the consistency of thin rubber cement when it is wet, and it is hard but still flexible when dry. It is usually applied with a syringe or squeeze bottle in narrow lines which outline and enclose color areas, like the lines in a coloring book. Dyes are either diluted and brushed on as washes of color, or used undiluted for vivid tones. Because the dye is brushed on the fabric, the colorations look like those in watercolor painting.

Acid dyes, prepared in a normal stock solution form, are excellent for this technique and offer an economical substitute for the specially marketed "silk dyes." The silk dyes are usually sold in a concentrated stock solution which includes water-soluble alcohol, to help the dye flow evenly and to speed drying. We recommend that you dilute your acid-dye stock solutions with a mixture of one part rubbing or denatured alcohol to one part water.

Be sure to work in a well-ventilated area. The dyes must be fixed with heat, and the gutta must be removed by dry cleaning when you are finished.

This technique is most effective on fine-weave silks, such as china silk, habutae, and silk broadcloth. Noil silks tend to be too heavy and textured for the gutta to penetrate evenly and produce an effective resist.

Equipment you will need:
- one measuring cup, with metric divisions
- storage bottles for dyes, capacity at least 50 ml
- one 10-ml syringe with needle (gauge 16, or about ¾ mm; available at veterinary supply; clip the point of the needle and file it smooth) **or** small squeeze bottle from dye supplier
- sketching tool
- small cups or watercolor trays, for mixing dyes
- wood stretcher frame, 14″ × 18″
- pushpins
- several small paint brushes
- canning kettle to be used as steamer to set the dye

Materials you will need:
- silk: hemmed scarves, and scraps for practice
- small amounts of basic colors of acid dye
- 5% acetic acid (white vinegar)
- rubbing (denatured) alcohol
- Gutta Serti
- thinner

Preparing the silk for painting:

Lay a portion of the silk over the stretcher frame. The scarf and the frame will probably be different sizes, so select an area to work, then move and re-pin the silk as necessary so you can apply gutta to all parts. After the gutta dries, move the silk and re-pin as necessary while you apply the dyes.

Pin the four center points of your working section, first pinning the left and right sides, then the top and bottom. Stretch the silk as you pin so it is taut, but don't strain the fabric. Then, stretching the fabric slightly to the right of the top pin and to the left of the bottom pin, secure the tightened fabric with two more pins, one inch to the right of the top pin and to the left of the bottom pin. Continue to work out from the center of both the top and the bottom, alternating sides until you reach both edges. Then do the same on the two sides, working out from the centers again.

Before you paint directly on silk, the fabric must be stretched on a frame. Begin with a pin on each of the four sides, stretching gently against the opposing pin to keep the fabric taut. Work out from the center with pins at 1″ intervals until the whole fabric is stretched on the frame.

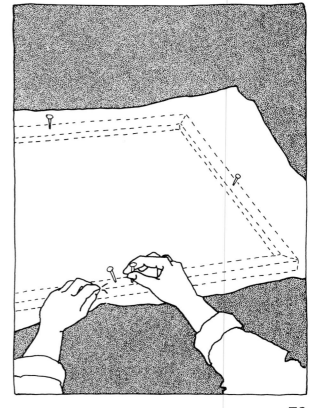

Project 8: Gutta-Resist Scarves. *Painting directly on silk is simplified with the use of gutta resist to hold each dye color in its own area. Paint yourself several scarves with wonderful watercolor effects.*

Lightly sketch the main features of your design on the silk, using the sketching tool.

Applying the gutta resist:

The gutta may need thinning. It should be the consistency of a raw egg, although you'll need to experiment to see what consistency works best for your purposes. Generally, you will use one part thinner to four parts gutta.

Fill the squeeze bottle or syringe with gutta. (If your bottle is new, you will need to pierce the tip with a needle to make a small hole.) Draw the outlines of your design with the gutta. Be sure all the spaces are completely enclosed and the lines are solid; the dyes can easily wick out of even the smallest spaces.

Applying the dye:

Mix 50 ml of stock solution for each dye color. Use ¼ tsp of dye in 50 ml of water. For pale colors, thin the stock solution with a 50/50 mix of water and denatured alcohol.

Your colors will be about half as dark if you dilute your dye 1-to-4 with the alcohol/water mix.

When the gutta is completely dry, brush in your dye colors. It is not necessary to paint right up to the gutta lines, since the dye will wick along the surface until it reaches the line. Paint fairly quickly to achieve smooth color areas, applying dye only to areas that are completely suspended in the frame and not touching the wood. Move the fabric when you need to.

Setting the dye:

A canning kettle with a rack makes an excellent steamer. After your fabric is completely dry, roll it in a piece of unprinted newsprint, to form a tube. Roll the tube so it becomes a fat, round package. Tie the roll securely, but not tightly.

Place the canning rack in the kettle, and fill to ¾ ″ below the rack with a mixture of ⅓ vinegar to ⅔

water. Cut a half dozen or so pieces of newsprint in circles 1″ smaller in diameter than the kettle; place three of them on the rack. Add the fabric bundle. Add another layer of several pieces of round newsprint. Check to be sure that none of the newsprint touches the walls of the kettle; if it comes in contact with water condensing on the wall of the steamer, the water will wick through the paper and onto the silk, causing the dye to run and splotch.

Put the lid carefully on the kettle. Increase the temperature until the liquid is steaming but not quite simmering. Steam for 15 minutes. Allow the kettle to cool just until you can handle the contents, then quickly remove the paper. If the paper is left on until the bundle is cold it may stick to the gutta.

When the fabric is completely cool, rinse it in warm water to remove any excess dye. Dry clean the fabric, to remove the gutta, before you press it.

Apply the gutta resist with a syringe or squeeze bottle, and let it dry. Then paint dye directly onto the fabric within the outlined areas.

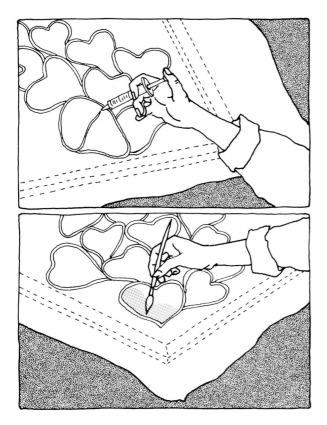

When a scarf is dry, remove it from the stretcher and roll it in unprinted paper. Set the acid dye by steaming above vinegar water, being careful to prevent water spots.

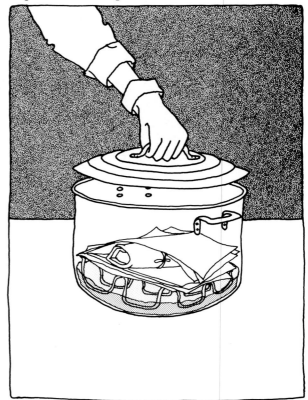

Project 9: Easy Ikat Table Runner

designed, dyed, and woven by Betsy Blumenthal

We've designed a relatively easy warp-ikat project to introduce you to this resist technique. If you want more information on this exciting dye method, we urge you to consult the resources listed in the appendix.

Our table runner uses just one ikat resist "spot" in its design. We added variety by shifting this spot into two positions on the warp, and by adding dyed and undyed background warpway stripes. We used the undyed cotton-linen yarn for the weft.

Equipment you will need for dyeing:
- one plastic dyepot
- two measuring cups, with metric divisions
- two 10-ml syringes
- plastic measuring spoons
- dishwashing gloves
- stir stick

Equipment you will need for ikat weaving:
- two C-clamps
- black permanent felt-tip marker
- two- or four-shaft floor loom, or rigid heddle loom, at least 18" wide
- 8-dent reed for floor loom (sley two ends per dent), or 16-e.p.i. rigid heddle
- two ¼"-diameter metal rods or wooden dowels, 18" long

Materials you will need:
- two small packages of fiber-reactive dye, one each in blue and black
- 1 ounce (2 tbsp) soda
- ¼ cup salt
- 1 pound of 8/4 unbleached cotton-linen blend, or similar cotton yarn, at about 92 yards/ounce (1600 yards/500 grams); we used Cot-lin from School Products
- one piece of cotton string, 4 feet long, for guide string
- plastic ikat tape, or strips of medium-weight plastic trash bags, for tying resist areas

Preparing the warps:
First we will wind the warps and tie the resist areas, then dye the warp chains. Prepare your warps as follows, using the diagram of the finished fabric for reference.
Warp length: 3 yards
Ends per inch: 16
Width in reed: 15½"
Total warp ends: 248
Yarn required for warp: 744 yards

Ikat warps: warp A = 24 ends; warp B = 32 ends.
Plain warps: warp C (background) = 168 ends; warp D (accent) = 24 ends.

Wind each warp separately, with a cross. First wind warp A and tie the cross loosely, then place several other loose ties along the warp. Place tight ties at the top and bottom ends. Without removing warp A from the board, wind warp B. Tie the cross and several loose ties in the same manner as A, and tie the top and bottom ends tightly as well. Then tie warps A and B together with loose ties at the beginnings, centers, and ends of the warps. Remove these two warps from the board. Wind warp C, tie it, and remove it from the board. Wind warp D, tie it, and remove it from the board.

Making the resist ties:
Stretch warps A and B together, using C-clamps placed three yards apart. Make a guide string to help you place the resist ties by marking 2" spots on a cotton string with a black permanent felt-tip marker, at 2" intervals. Tie the guide string to the C-clamps, parallel to the warp yarns.

Tie a 2" resist spot every 2" along the warp; use a 1"-wide plastic strip about 12" long for each tie. Hold the spot to be wrapped very tightly with one hand, and wrap securely. Stretch the plastic firmly, and overlap each wrap generously with the next until

Tie warps A and B loosely together while still on the warping board, in addition to the normal ties on each skein. Stretch them between C-clamps and add a marking thread to show where the ties should be.

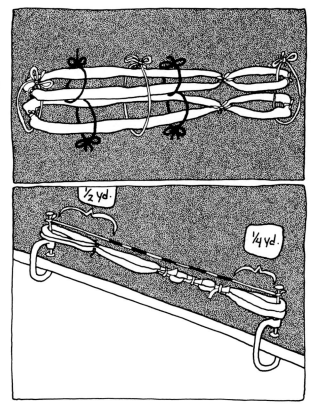

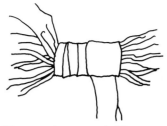

the 2" space is covered. Then wrap both ends of the plastic tie back toward the center of the resist area and firmly tie the ends together.

Following the guide string, wrap 22 spots in this manner. Leave ½ yard at the cross end of the warp, and ¼ yard at the other end. This part of the warp will be used to tie the warp to the loom and will not be woven.

The dye run:

Only one dyepot is required for this project. The amount of fiber in the pot can be determined as follows: Warps A and B will weigh about 50 grams total (168 yards = 1.7 oz. = 50 gm). Since only the un-wrapped half of this warp will be exposed to the dye, use half of 50 grams, or 25 grams, as the weight of goods for this warp. Warp D weighs slightly more than ½ ounce, or about 15 grams. These three warps combined (A plus B plus D) total 40 grams. For a medium shade on this much fiber, you will need 20 ml of stock solution (see page 23).

Wash and rinse all four warps. Remove warp C and hang it up to dry. It will not be dyed, but is washed so that all the warp yarns are similarly preshrunk. Leave warps A, B, and D to wet out for 20 minutes while you prepare the dyepot.

Mix 25 ml stock solution of each color, using ¼ tsp of dye in 25 ml of water for each (see page 22). Put 10 ml of each color into the dyepot. (An alternate method avoids wasted dye and yields a slightly darker color. Mix ⅛ tsp of each dye together in 20 ml water and use the entire mixture in the dyebath.)

Add 1 liter of hot water and 4 tsp of salt to the pot. Add the wetted-out

warps (A, B, and D) to the pot and stir gently for 15 minutes. Mix 2 tsp fixer (sodium carbonate) in 20 ml hot water until the soda dissolves. Remove the warps from the dyepot, add the fixer, stir, and return the warps to the pot. Continue to stir occasionally for 45 minutes more. Pour off the dye, rinse the warps, and hang them to dry. When they

dried, remove the plastic ties, and separate warps A and B.

Dressing the loom:

Take special care to avoid disrupting the warp-ikat yarns. These instructions are written for a floor loom, but can be easily adapted for a rigid heddle.

Warp order plan

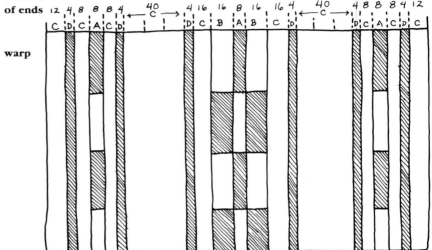

Working with all four warps at once and using the cross end of each warp, slide the appropriate number of warp ends onto a pair of lease sticks, alternating warps so the stripes end up as shown in the warp diagram above. Then slide a dowel into the loops of warps A, C, and D. Lash this dowel firmly to the back apron rod of your loom. Slip another dowel through the loops of warp B and lash this bar to the apron rod so that it lies 2" forward of the other dowel. This offsets the ikat spots.

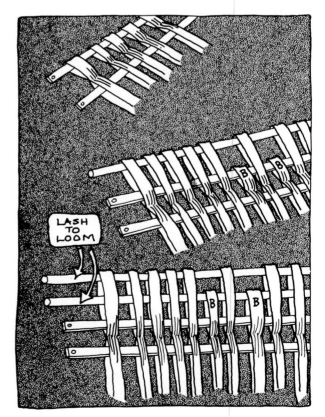

LASH TO LOOM

1. Attach the four warps to the back apron as follows: working with all four warps at once and using the cross end of each warp, slide the appropriate number of warp ends onto a pair of lease sticks, alternating warps so the stripes line up as shown in the warp diagram. You will use 12 ends of warp C, then 4 ends of warp D, 8 ends of C, 8 ends of A, 8 ends of C, 4 ends of D, and so forth, until the crosses for all the warps have been transferred to the lease sticks in the order shown.

2. Slide one of the 18″ dowels through all the loops at the cross ends of warps A, C, and D *only,* leaving warp B unattached for the moment. Lash this dowel firmly to the back apron rod. Now place the other dowel through the loops at the cross end of warp B and lash this dowel onto the back apron rod so it lies 2″ forward of the first dowel. This will shift the ikat resist spots on warp B and will align the ikat pattern.

3. Keeping the lease sticks in place, wind the warp onto the back

Comb as little as possible, to avoid shifting the ikat spots out of position.

4. Thread the heddles and the reed, and tie on.

Weaving the table runner:

This is the easy part. Your pattern is complete and waiting on your warp. Use plain weave throughout, with the unbleached 8/4 cotton-linen for weft. After removing the runner from the loom, finish the ends with a small knotted fringe, or with hem-stitching.

Project 9: Easy Ikat Table Runner. *An easy technique offsets the dyed spots for this beautiful table runner.*

Project 10. Fold-dye Scarves, Shirts, and Other Items. *A fun family dye project produced these lovely scarves as well as colorful clothing for the whole family.*

Project 10: Fold-dye Scarves, Shirts, and Other Items

designed and dyed by Betsy, Dana, and Gregory Blumenthal

Fold-dyeing is one type of tie-dyeing, a simple yet powerful design technique for home dyers. The process is easy, and results are interesting and exciting, even for beginners. We've seen children aged 3 to 16 spend many happy hours creating original designs on their own clothing.

Fiber-reactive dyes are ideal, since they are permanent, yield bright colors on cotton, silk, and wool, and are relatively inexpensive and easy to obtain. You can mix stock solutions from powdered fiber-reactive dyes (as our instructions indicate) or purchase the liquid form. Liquid union dyes also work, although the colors will not be as fast.

In this project we combined two dye tricks: fold-dye resist areas and rainbow application of dyes. *Fold-dyeing* is a simple resist technique; fabric is folded in a pattern which creates several superimposed layers of cloth. The sections of fabric inside the folds resist the dye, but the color penetrates the layers to make a repeat pattern. *Rainbow dyeing* is a term used to describe direct application of dyes, as opposed to the more usual immersion (or dyepot) technique.

Several colors of stock solutions of dyes are painted, dumped, poured, or squirted onto the fabric.

You can overdye colored items or work with white goods, as you prefer. If you begin with colored fabric, remember that its color will affect the colors of your finished cloth.

First, you wet out the fabric in a pre-soak solution of salt and fixer. Then you fold the fabric according to a plan (see suggestions). Next you apply dye—we put several colors on different sections of our folded bundle, using full-strength stock solutions, and left the dyed bundle covered (we wrapped it in plastic) for several hours to set the dye. When we could wait no longer, we rinsed each item under running water, and unfolded the bundle to reveal the multicolored results.

We've included some of our favorite ideas to inspire you, although we guarantee that your products will not look just like ours. No matter how hard you try, no two tie-dye projects ever come out exactly the same.

Equipment you will need:

- plastic dishpan or dyepot, for pre-soaking fiber
- several 10-ml syringes, one for each color of dye
- bottles for stock solutions, about 500 ml capacity, one for each color of dye
- squirt bottles: use old detergent bottles and the like—spray bottles are fun if you are working outside, but are too messy for inside
- disposable plastic plates
- plastic bags, bread-bag size
- one pair of dishwashing gloves for each participant
- a sheet of plastic, to cover working surfaces
- *(for wool fibers only)* an enamel pot, or microwave casserole, for heat-setting dye

Materials you will need:

- a collection of 100% cotton, silk, or wool shirts, scarves, pants, and so forth; if your item is not 100% natural fiber you will get paler colors, since only the natural-fiber portion will accept the dye
- rubber bands or string, for tying bundles of fiber

Weigh the clean, dry, cellulose-fiber items separately from the protein-fiber items to find the weight of goods for each dyebath.

- one small package of fiber-reactive dye for each color; we used Ciba-cron F Red, Yellow, Orange, Lemon Yellow, Purple, Turquoise, and Navy.
- 1 cup (½ pound) salt for every pound of fiber
- *(for cotton and silk)* ½ cup fixer (sodium carbonate) for every pound of fiber, to set dyes
- *(for wool)* 2 cups 5% acetic acid (white vinegar) for every pound of fiber, to set dyes

Preparing the materials:

Weigh the collected fabrics that you plan to dye, separating any wool items from the cotton and silk ones. Silk can be dyed with either the wool or the cotton method. We used the cotton process for our silk scarves.

Wash any new items thoroughly to remove sizing. Be sure that used items are clean and free of grease spots.

Pre-soak your materials as follows: Using the weight of your materials as a basis, figure out how much salt and fixer you need in your pre-soak solu-tion and prepare the solution. If you have more or less material than a pound, adjust the proportions of salt and fixer to match.

—*For every pound of cotton and silk,* mix 1 cup of salt and ½ cup of fixer in 2 gallons of warm water (or enough water to cover your fabric). Add fabric and soak for 30 minutes.

—*For every pound of wool,* mix ½ cup of salt and 2 cups of vinegar in 2 gallons of warm water (or enough water to cover your fabric). Add fabric and soak for 30 minutes.

Preparing the dye:

Mix between 200 and 400 ml of stock solution for each color you plan to use. Use the regular recipe for fiber-reactive dyes (1 tsp dye to 100 ml of water; see pages 38–39). Since you will not add the fixer to the dye, you can save any leftover solution.

If you want intense colors, use between 400 and 600 ml of stock solution for every pound of fabric. For pastel colors, use only 100 to 150 ml of stock solution and dilute it 4–to–1 with water; in other words, use 20 ml of regular stock solution in 80 ml of water, for 100 ml of dilute stock solution.

The dye run:

Now the fun begins. Working on your plastic-coated surface, choose a fold plan and prepare your fabric for dyeing. For some ideas, see the sketches of plans we played with. Add rubber bands or ties to hold your bundles together, although the wet fabric often stays in place with-out ties.

The dye is applied the same way for all fibers—cotton, silk, or wool. Place the fabric on a plate to catch the drips. If you want to keep the bottom of your bundle from being contaminated with a mix of dripping colors, use a rack or several layers of folded paper towel to lift the fabric off the plate.

Squirt, dump, or pour dye onto the bundle. You may want random effects, or you may want to plan for a particular result. You can turn your bundle over and apply colors to the other side, or to each of four sides,

Presoak your wool items in a vinegar-and-salt solution, and your cotton or silk items in a soda-and-salt solution.

Working with your wet items on a plastic-covered table, fold them into various patterns. Hold the folds with rubberbands or ties.

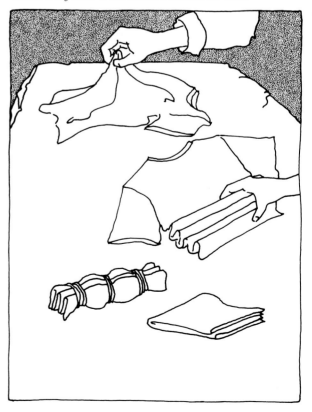

or whatever you choose. Unless you want toned colors, avoid overlapping more than two colors of dye at any point—any mix of three primary hues produces a brown- or gray-toned color.

When your bundle looks well saturated with dye, you are done. The cloth should look very dark, almost black, in places. Not all of the dye will fix to the fiber, and your finished product will be significantly lighter when rinsed and washed.

You'll fix the dye differently if you're working with cotton and silk, or with wool. For cottons and silks, all you have to do is wrap the bundle in a plastic bag and let it soak for several hours or overnight. The longer you leave it the more intense your colors will be, although the amount of additional intensity gained after three hours is small.

Wool requires heat. Place the bundle of wool fabrics on a rack in a dyepot, cover the pot, and steam the fabric for 15 minutes; or place the bundle in a covered microwave casserole and microwave for 5 to 10 minutes on high. Be sure that the fiber steams for at least 5 minutes, and that there is enough moisture to keep the fiber from scorching. Leave the cloth to cool to room temperature, or overnight, with the cover on.

Washing and rinsing tie-dyes:

Whether you work with cotton, silk, or wool, it is important to rinse your bundles quickly so each section of your design will not be contaminated with dye from other sections.

First rinse your bundle in warm running water while it is still folded: rinse one corner at a time, holding the rest out of the way so the excess dye does not wash over it. Gently squeeze to remove the dye. Work along the bundle until most of the extra dye has rinsed off.

Unfold the bundle, and rinse until the water runs clear.

Finally, wash your fiber, and rinse again. Some unfixed dye may still wash out during this final stage, but there will not be enough dye or fixer left for one section to contaminate another at this point.

Line dry and admire!

Place your bundled fabric on a plate, and squirt or pour dye solution onto it. When it looks saturated with dye, it is ready to be set. Put fabrics from the cellulose batch into individual plastic bags and let them sit overnight to set. Fabrics from the protein batch must be steamed as explained on page 75.

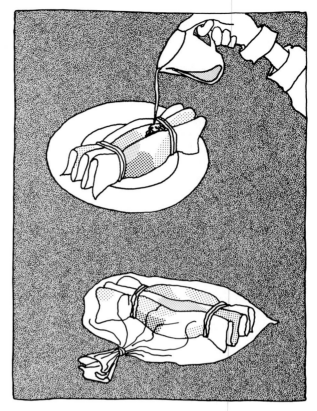

Project 11: Rainbow-dyed Fleece, for Handspun Handknit Hat and Mittens

designed, spun and knit by Anne Wulf—dyed by Betsy Blumenthal

Rainbow dyeing is an excellent way to achieve exciting multicolor effects on yarns, fabrics, or fleece. With this technique you usually intend to get random blocks of color, although precise results are also possible.

We particularly liked our rainbow-dyed fleece. In one easy dye run, we created a "fleece of many colors," from which we then spun multicolor yarn. The way our yarn looked depended on how we applied the dye, how we prepared the fleece for spinning, and how we controlled the colors as we spun.

For this project we dyed white fleece in the three primary shades of red, blue, and yellow, and then made a yarn which used these three colors in rotation and also allowed them to blend, to produce secondary colors. We knit a hat and mitten set with our multicolor yarn.

We used acid dye on wool, so we needed to heat-set our dyes. In Method 1, we used a regular dyepot on the stove. In Method 2, we used a microwave oven and a covered casserole.

Equipment you will need:
Both methods:
- one measuring cup, with metric divisions
- plastic measuring spoons
- dishwashing gloves

Method 1:
- enamel (or other nonreactive) dyepot, at least 2 gallon capacity
- stove

Method 2:
- casserole dish, 2 quart capacity
- microwave oven

Materials you will need (both methods):
- ½ pound (about 250 grams) of fleece
- one small package of each color of acid dye you will use: we used Yellow, Red, and Blue
- ½ cup (¼ pound) salt
- 2 cups (500 ml) 5% acetic acid (white vinegar)

Preparing the materials:
Gently wash and rinse the fleece in lukewarm water. Prepare a pre-soak solution of salt and fixer, by dissolving ¼ cup salt and 500 ml vinegar in ½ gallon (2 liters) of water. Gently squeeze the rinse water from the wet fleece and submerge the fleece in this pre-soak solution. Allow to wet out for 15 minutes while you prepare the stock solutions.

Preparing the dye:
Use the standard proportions for acid dye to prepare 100 ml of stock solution in each of the three colors (½ tsp of dye to 100 ml of water; see pages 22 and 40).

The dye run:
Method 1: To avoid having the dye colors mix on the bottom, place a rack in the dyepot. Remove the fleece from the pre-soak solution, saving the extra solution, and gently squeeze out the excess liquid. Place the fleece in the dyepot. Pour one of the colors randomly onto a third of the fleece, the second color onto another third, and the third color onto the last third. Allow the colors to mix at their borders. With gloved hands, press down gently on the fleece to force the dye into the lower layers. Place the dyepot on the stove, cover it, and slowly raise the heat to a simmer over the next 15 minutes. Do not stir. The drips from the wet fleece and the liquid of the dye will provide enough moisture to make steam. Check occasionally to be sure that some liquid remains in the bottom of the pot, as a source of steam. If the pot becomes too dry it will burn. If you need more moisture, add some of the pre-soak solution. Simmer for 45 minutes. Turn off the heat and allow the dyepot to cool to room temperature. Rinse the fleece in lukewarm water, working very carefully to avoid felting the wool (do not press too hard or agitate the wool). Spread the dyed fleece on a rustproof rack or screen to dry.

Method 2: Prepare the dyepot as in Method 1, but use a microwave casserole in place of the dyepot. If possible, use a plastic rack in the bottom of the casserole. Apply the dye as above. Cover and cook in the microwave on high for 5 minutes, or until the liquid simmers. Check to be sure some liquid remains in the casserole, and cook on high for an additional 5 minutes. Leave covered and cool to room temperature. Rinse and dry as in Method 1.

Spinning the fleece:
For our project, you will need about 6 ounces (600 yards) of two-ply multicolor sportweight wool. In addition to the multicolor yarn, we spun about 2 ounces (200 yards) of white mohair to use as an accent yarn. This is more yarn than we actually needed, but gave us leeway to experiment with the pattern and the placement of colors.

There are two basic approaches to spinning multicolor fleece: you can try for an overall blended or "heather" effect, or you can spin with less color mixing to make a yarn which changes color randomly. We used the latter approach, although we describe both methods so you can choose for yourself.

Heather effect: Card the wool with hand cards or a carding machine. Keep your final color even by putting the same amount of each of your colors on the cards every time. Even with a great deal of practice, however, you will get some color variation between the rolags. We feel these minor inconsistencies add to the character of the final product.

Random multicolor effect: First isolate your dyed colors from each other as much as possible. Instead of carding, carefully tease each color separately with your fingers. Then select a small amount of each color, until you are holding the equivalent of a rolag in your hand. As you spin, alternate the colors in your hand so that as you draw out the wool you produce several inches of each color before you blend into the next. The blending of colors will occur without effort as you proceed, and lots of exciting mixes of your colors will appear on the bobbin.

Knitting the hat and mittens:

You first need to determine the gauge at which you want to knit your yarn. We spun to a small diameter, making a yarn with about 100 yards per ounce. We knit a trial swatch of 20 stitches by 20 rows, using size 4 needles; the gauge was 6 stitches/inch and 8 rows/inch.

The instructions here are for a women's medium-size hat and mittens with a gauge of 6 stitches per inch. If your wool knits to a different gauge, you can easily adapt our patterns. An average adult head is 22″ in circumference. An average hat for this size is knit 1″ smaller for a close fit, or 21″. Multiply your stitch gauge by 21″ to get the number of stitches required for an average hat, and round up or down as necessary to get a multiple of four for the K2, P2

rib *and* a multiple of six to work with the Fair Isle pattern sections. If your number is not initially divisible by both four and six, adjust the number of stitches on the fourth row, as we did for our hat. When changing to another gauge, adjust the number of rows as well, by adding or subtracting rows in the unpatterned area, so you come out with a hat between 11″ and 12″ in overall height. A standard mitten is between 7″ and 8″ in diameter, and 10″ long; use these measurements to adjust the mitten pattern in the same manner.

Pattern stitch, for brim of hat and cuff of mitten: Follow the chart for placement of colors and popcorn stitches. Work the popcorn stitch at places indicated in the chart, using the multicolor yarn, as follows: Make 3 new stitches out of one stitch by knitting first into the front of the stitch, then in the back, and then in the front again. Turn the work and purl these 3 stitches. Turn, K3; turn, P3; turn, slip 1, K2 tog, PSSO (pass the slip stitch over). Popcorn stitch is complete; continue with row.

Hat

Brim: Using size 4 circular needles (or size required to obtain gauge of 6

stitches/inch), cast on 128 stitches, using the multicolor yarn. Join work, placing marker on needle to indicate the start of each round. Work K2, P2 rib for four rounds, decreasing 2 sts on the last round (126 sts). Change to white yarn and K three rounds. Add the multicolor yarn and work Pattern I (see chart) for nine rounds. Drop multicolor yarn and with white K one round, then K1, P1 rib for two rounds. Pick up multicolor yarn and K1, P1 rib for ten rounds. End brim by using white in K1, P1 rib for ten rounds.

Reverse round: In order for the brim of the hat to be right side out when it is folded up, you will need to switch from "outside" to "inside" at this point. This is done by simply reversing the direction you are knitting on your circular needle.

Cap: Continuing with white yarn, work in stockinette stitch for 2″. Add the multicolor yarn and work the next three rounds in Pattern II (see chart). Drop the white yarn and work in stockinette for another 2″.

Decrease for top: *K2 tog, K2 tog, P2*, repeat around. With multicolor, work K2, P2 rib for 2½″. Decrease in last round: *K2 tog, P2 tog*, repeat around. Break yarn, leaving a 12″ tail. Thread the remaining stitches on the tail and pull tight. Sew firmly with a backstitch to secure yarn; trim extra yarn off. Make a pompom and attach it, if you want.

Mittens

These instructions are for a mitten which fits both right and left hands. Make two. Using a set of four double-pointed needles, size 4, cast on 48 stitches, using the multicolor yarn. Join and knit cuff exactly as for brim of hat, through row 9 of Pattern I. Drop the multicolor. Working with white, knit one round, then K1, P1 rib for two rounds. Change to multicolor and K1, P1 rib for four rounds. Repeat these six rounds (two of white, four of multicolor) in rib once, then end with K1, P1 rib in white for two rounds.

Increase for thumb: Knit next round in white yarn and stockinette, placing two markers—one between the first and second stitches at the start of the round, and the other between the next-to-last and last stitches in each round. Increase 2 sts 8 times for thumb, by increasing 1 st in the stitch before the first marker,

Presoak the fleece, squeeze out excess liquid, and put it on a rack in a large pan. Pour dye directly onto the fleece, using different colors in different sections. Press down to force the dye into the lower layer, then steam-set the dye.

and 1 st in the stitch after the second marker in every other round. *At the same time,* after six rounds of increase, add the multicolor yarn on the increase round (a total of 54 sts) and work Pattern II on the next three rounds. To avoid extra stitches on the thumb, suspend the increase due on round three of the pattern, and work it on the following round instead. Drop the white yarn and knit with the multicolor yarn, continuing to increase every other round until you have finished the 8 sets of increases and have a total of 64 sts. Place 16 sts of the 18 which are between the markers on a stitch holder or thread, to reserve for the thumb, leaving the 2 sts right next to the markers as part of the "hand."

Hand: With multicolor yarn, knit four rounds on the 48 sts remaining for the hand. Add white yarn and work Pattern II in reverse for three rounds. Drop the multicolor. Work in stockinette with white until mitten is 8″ long, or desired length minus 3″, measuring from cast-on round. Add multicolor and work Pattern II for three rounds. Drop white and work stockinette in multicolor for four rounds.

Decrease for top: *K1, K2 tog, K18, K2 tog, K1*, repeat once. Knit one round without decreases. Then *K1, K2 tog, K16, K2 tog, K1*, repeat once. Knit one round without decreases. Continue to decrease 4 sts on every other round in this manner until 10 sts remain on each side. Place 10 sts on each of two needles so that the decreases line up at the sides, and weave sts together with kitchener stitch or knit together and cast off across. (If latter method is used, reverse the mitten before casting off, so cast-off ridge is on the inside.)

Thumb: Pick up the 16 sts left for the thumb, pick up 2 additional sts from hand of mitten just inside thumb, and distribute these 18 sts evenly on three needles. Work Pattern II in reverse for three rounds, then white only for four rounds, then Pattern II again. Knit with multicolor until thumb measures 2″ or desired length, then decrease for top of thumb: *K1, K2 tog*, around. Knit one round without decreases. Repeat decrease on following two rounds until 6 sts remain. Place these sts on two needles, 3 per needle, and bind off as for hand. Weave in loose ends.

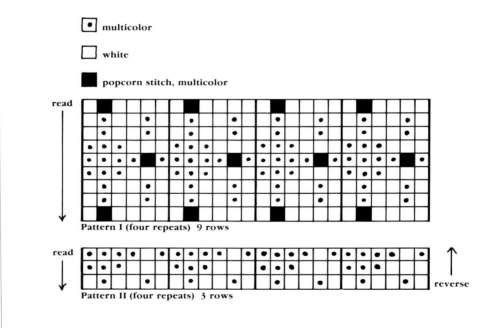

multicolor

white

popcorn stitch, multicolor

read

Pattern I (four repeats) 9 rows

read   reverse

Pattern II (four repeats) 3 rows

Project 11. Rainbow-dyed Fleece, for Handspun, Handknit Hat and Mittens. *Spinners will love working with this multicolor fleece, made in one quick and easy dyebath.*

Tapestry Rug *by Betsy Blumenthal*

8

Overdyeing for Color Families

An exciting extension of home dyeing is overdyeing. An existing color overdyed with another color results in a third color. This third color is similar to the color which would have been obtained had the two colors of dye been mixed before dyeing. For example, if your original fiber is red, overdyeing it with blue will make it purple; overdyeing it with orange will produce red-orange; and overdyeing with green will result in brown.

There are several simple color rules to remember when overdyeing.

1. A primary color can never be overdyed to become another primary color. Similarly, you cannot create any overdyed color which does not contain the original color of your fiber. For example, you cannot create orange from a blue fiber since orange is made only of yellow and red, and contains no blue. A possible exception to this rule is if the blue color of the original fiber is very pale. In this case the color that is already in the fiber serves as a toner. For example, an overdye of a strong orange on a pale blue will produce a rusty or browned-out orange.

2. If a color is overdyed by its complement, the original color will be toned down toward brown.

3. Overdyeing fibers cannot result in lighter values than the original color. A medium blue can become darker but cannot be modified to become a paler blue.

4. Plan your overdyeing as if you were mixing the colors before dyeing. Use the color wheel and the color sphere in Chapter 5 for guidance.

Overdyeing for sets of harmonious colors

You may have fabrics or yarns that you purchased some time ago in colors that are no longer useful or appealing, or you may have colors that you have already dyed and wish to change. These fibers are candidates for overdyeing. In Project 12, we overdyed some very used blue jeans before weaving them into a unique rag rug. The jeans were dyed as if they were white cotton fabric. The faded denim color gave a blue undertone to the newly dyed colors.

Using this same concept, you can coordinate a disparate collection of leftover pieces of yarn or fabric. For example, calicos can be unified for a suitable collection of quilting fabrics.

Overdyeing to unify a mixed collection of colors is most successful if the colors to be overdyed are closely related on the color wheel. For example, lilac and orange are related because they both have red as a component, so they can be unified with an overdye of red. On the other hand, lilac and yellow would be difficult to unify with an overdye run because they are opposite on the color wheel, and an attempt to unify them with an overdye of any color would tend to produce muddy tones on at least one of the original colors.

Overdyeing to subdue colors

It is often desirable to overdye colors in order to only slightly modify or "tone" them. A group of very bright unharmonious colors are synchronized when overdyed with a small amount of a toner. Toners are a mixture of all three primary colors, and are therefore some form of brown or black. For example, a *warm*, or brown, toner, one that leans toward warm colors (yellow-orange-red), could be made of 3 parts red, 4 parts yellow, and 3 parts blue. A *cool*, or black, toner (which leans toward purple-blue-green) could be made of 4 parts blue, 3 parts yellow, and 2 parts red. These toners can be mixed from the stock solutions and then used in small quantities to reduce the brightness of the original colors. Overdyeing with toners makes colors seem more natural and earthy.

Double-dyeing: An overdye system for multiple colors

An exciting and relatively unknown extension of overdyeing is a system for producing a large number of related colors with only a few dyebaths. We call this system double-dyeing because we dye each skein of yarn or piece of fabric twice to obtain the final results. Here's an overview of how the system works.

Several dyepots are set up for a dye run. However, instead of having just one piece of fabric or skein of yarn in each pot, we put several skeins or pieces into each pot. When this first dye run is complete, we shuffle the fibers into multicolor groups, and re-dye or overdye each group together in a second pot. When the second dye run is complete, we obtain several colors from each pot of the second run, and therefore a large number of colors from all of the second pots. From relatively few dyepots, we have created a large batch of related colors.

To better understand this system, consider the following specific example. First, several skeins of yarn or pieces of fabric are dyed in four steps of a value gradation. For example, four different values of blue (pale, light, medium, and dark) are dyed, with four skeins of yarn or four pieces of fabric in each pot. After this initial dye run is complete, the skeins or fabrics are sorted into four groups, with one representative from each of the first dye run's four blue value steps in each new group. At this point the groups are considered to be single units, and the fact that they are a combination of different colors of blue is ignored. Now the first group is overdyed with a pale value of another color, say red, and the second group is overdyed with a light red, the third group with a medium red, and the fourth group with a dark red. When the second dye run is complete, there will be four distinct shades of purple yarn or fabric in each pot, for a total of sixteen different purple colors from only eight dyepots! If we had dyed five different values in each dye run, for a total of ten dyepots in both runs, we would have had twenty-five (5 by 5) distinct colors in hand at the end.

This method of dyeing works only with dyes that are non-reversible. Of the dyes covered in this book, the pre-metallized dyes and the fiber-reactive dyes qualify. The acid dyes and most union dyes are reversible.

The discussion in Chapter 4 explains reversibility, and you can check there to be sure the dye you are planning to use for a double-dye run is non-reversible before you begin.

If you want to determine for yourself whether or not a dyestuff is reversible, use the following test. Select sample amounts of fiber which have been dyed with the dye in question, in several colors which represent a wide color spectrum. Set a snip of each color aside for comparison at the end of the test. Add an undyed piece of fiber to your colors, and weigh (or estimate the weight of) the bundle. Wet out the pieces in a dyepot. Add the chemical assistants which would be required for a regular dye run of the dye in question. Run your samples through a complete "dye run," with everything except dye —heat if necessary and work the fibers for the full amount of time. Rinse and dry your samples. Compare them to the original color snips, and see if the undyed piece has taken up any color.

All dyestuffs will reverse to some extent, so you can expect that the undyed piece will be at least pale gray or brown. If your colors have mostly remained distinct from each other and are only somewhat toned down in comparison to their starting colors, then your dyestuff is suitable for overdyeing. Conversely, if you now have a uniform collection of muddy colors, you should reject the dyestuff for overdyeing and double-dyeing.

Naturally, the best way to really understand the double-dye system is to try it. Project 13 is a double-dye run with fiber-reactive dyes on cotton fabric.

The double-dye system requires some careful planning, but the results justify the extra time since this system yields lots of colors from a few dyebaths. When you want to set up a double-dye run of your own, you will need to know how many skeins of yarn or pieces of fabric to prepare. In addition, you will need to know the total quantity of fiber that will be in each dyepot in order to calculate the correct amounts of dye and assistants. We offer the following somewhat mathematical discussion as a guideline.

To calculate your own double-dye run, first decide on the number of steps to be dyed in each of the two dye runs, and the colors to be used. You can use value steps, as we did in Project 13, or you can choose several steps of a hue or two-color gradation. For example, instead of a value progression of pale to dark orange, you could start with four steps of a yellow-to-red hue gradation for your first dye run. Similarly, you could use a two-color gradation for the second dye run's set of dyepots, too. Whatever colors you pick for your first and second dye runs, the numbers of skeins or pieces of fabric required are always worked out in the same way. To simplify the explanation, we will refer to the color or colors you use in the first dye run as color A, and the color or colors you use in the second dye run as color B.

Suppose you choose a three-step gradation crossed with another three-step gradation. This will yield nine colors ($3 \times 3 = 9$) in six dyepots ($3 + 3 = 6$). If you choose a four-step gradation crossed with a five-step gradation, this will yield 20 colors ($4 \times 5 = 20$) in 9 dyepots ($4 + 5 = 9$).

You will need to plan for one skein or piece of fabric for each finished color, plus one extra for each pot. This extra piece in each pot is never overdyed, and serves as a reference or control. You will have a control skein for each pot in the first dye run, and one for each pot in the second dye run. In a 4×5 cross, you will need 20 units for the color cross, and an additional 9 for the controls, or a total of 29 skeins or pieces of fabric.

You will need to calculate the water, dye, and chemical assistants for your first and second dye runs according to the total weight of fibers in each dyebath. Using the 4×5 cross from above as an example, this is worked out as follows: You will first dye 4 steps of color A. Into each dyebath you will place 5 skeins or fabrics for each of the 5 steps to be dyed in color B, plus 1 skein or fabric for a control, for a total of 6 skeins or fabrics per dyebath. Suppose, for example, that each skein of yarn or piece of fabric weighs 25 grams. Then each dyebath in the first round will contain 6×25 grams, or 150 grams. You will use this total weight of goods as a base to calculate the amount of dye and chemicals required.

To continue with our example, in the second dye run, when you overdye with 5 steps of color B you will have 5 dyepots, each of which will contain 4 skeins of yarn or pieces of fabric from the first run plus one extra undyed skein or fabric for a second dye run control, for a total of 5 units per dyebath. At 25 grams per unit, the second dyebaths will each contain a total of 125 grams. This weight of goods will be used to calculate the amounts of dye and chemicals required for the second dye run.

As you can see, if you have the same number of value steps in the second dye run as you have in the first, for example, if your dye run is a 4×4 color cross instead of a 4×5 cross, these calculations will only have to be done once instead of twice. You may want to take this into consideration to reduce the effort in your double-dye run.

It may seem that a double-dye run is too complicated to be worth the time and effort. We recommend that you try it at least once before you come to any firm conclusion. Like most techniques, it is an excellent way to achieve a certain type of result. It is, for example, not the best way to get a small number of intense colors. It is, however, an excellent method of producing a mass of closely related colors.

Double-dyeing is the last in the series of dye techniques which we have covered in this book. Unlike the others it is a relatively uncharted territory. Just like the others, it is worth a lot of further experimentation.

Project 12: Blue Jeans Rag Rug

designed, dyed and woven by Claire Kiehle

The enduring popularity of rag rugs is well deserved. These sturdy, washable accent rugs can be made from scraps and require only a minimum of time to weave. Our version is made from old blue jeans, overdyed in vivid shades of fuchsia, yellow, and turquoise. These colors are echoed in the rug warp, which is made of red, blue, and yellow cotton. A classic block threading known as *log cabin weave* is used to unify the overall design. This is a plain weave in which the light (red in this case) and dark (blue) threads alternate in both warp and weft to form blocks which can be woven in patterns. We used our third color, yellow, as an accent to separate the blocks.

The materials we specify will be enough for two rugs, each 25″ × 40″, plus fringe.

Equipment you will need:
- three large plastic dye buckets, capacity at least 6 gallons
- one measuring cup with metric divisions, capacity at least 250 ml
- plastic measuring spoons
- stir sticks (sturdy!)
- dishwashing gloves
- loom, at least 25″ weaving width and at least two shafts

Materials you will need:
- 3 pounds of used blue jean fabric, one pound for each of our three colors; we found that two pairs of women's size 12–14 jeans yield about one pound of fabric
- one small package of fiber-reactive dye (about 1 tbsp) each of Fuchsia, Turquoise, and Lemon Yellow; we used Cibacron Fuchsia F-35, Turquoise F-40, and Lemon Yellow F-11, from Pro-Chem
- 1 pound salt
- ½ pound fixer (sodium carbonate)
- three 8-ounce tubes of 8/4 cotton carpet warp, at 1600 yards per pound: one tube each of red, blue, and yellow; you will need about 700 yards of red, 700 yards of blue, and 400 yards (260 yards for warp plus 140 yards for weft) of yellow carpet warp.

Preparing the materials:
Wash and wet out the blue jeans. It is easiest to use a washing machine for this; leave the jeans to soak in the machine's tub or in a separate basin while you prepare the dye.

Preparing the dyepots:
For a medium depth of color on 1 pound (about 500 gm) of fiber, you will need 250 ml of stock solution. Since you will be using only one color in each dyepot it is not necessary to mix a carefully measured stock solution.

The usual amount of dye you would use to make 250 ml of stock solution would be 2½ tsp; you can instead make a paste of about 1 tbsp of dye in about 20 ml of water (a tablespoon is actually three teaspoons' worth). Use your measuring cup to make the paste, then add water to the 250-ml line.

Pour this concentrated dye solution directly into the dyepot and rinse the cup several times, adding the rinse liquid to the dyepot. Repeat this process for each of your colors. Then add 4 gallons of water and 1 cup of salt to each pot, and stir well.

The dye run:
Add one-third of the wet blue jeans (about 1 pound dry weight) to each dyepot. Stir well for 15 minutes. If you have long, sturdy gloves, it is easiest to stir with your hands. At the 15-minute mark, working with one pot at a time, prepare the fixer by mixing ½ cup fixer in 1 cup of hot water; stir until dissolved. Remove the fabric, add the fixer, and reimmerse the fabric. Repeat for the other two dyebaths. Stir occasionally for the next 45 minutes. In this project, even dyeing is not important, so lots of stirring is not necessary.

For the darkest possible colors, you can leave the jeans in the dyepot for several hours or overnight. When the dye run is complete, rinse the cloth thoroughly, then wash and rinse it again. Hang it up to dry.

Preparing the jeans fabric for weft:
Remove the waistbands, zippers, pockets, and so forth from the jeans. Cut the legs in spirals, to yield one large ball of weft per leg. The exact width of the strip you cut will depend on the weight of your jeans. To determine an appropriate width, fold a sample strip in half and twist it firmly; you want it to end up about as thick as a pencil.

Weaving the rug:
Log cabin is a plain weave structure with two different sections, or blocks, which alternate to form the pattern. Each block is threaded with alternating colors of warp, as listed in the color plan below. In our version, we added an accent block of all-yellow warps.

There are two wefts, the heavy blue jeans weft and the thinner cotton carpet yarn, which alternate throughout.

Warp length: 4 yards (enough for two rugs)

Ends per inch: 16, double-sleyed in an 8-dent reed

Width in reed: 25¼″

Total warp ends: 404 (red 170, blue 170, yellow 64)

Color plan:

Block A—shaft 1 blue, shaft 2 red for 20 ends

Block B—shaft 1 red, shaft 2 blue for 20 ends

Block C—solid yellow on both shafts for 4 ends

Repeat blocks A, B, and C across the warp as follows: *Block A, Block C, Block B, Block C*. Repeat 8 times, then end with one repeat of Block A.

Wind two warps, one with red and blue held together and the other with just yellow. Thread the loom from front to back, with one red and one blue in each dent of the reed for Blocks A and B, and with four yellow threads inserted in pairs for Block C. When you thread the heddles with the ends coming from the reed, take care to reverse the order of the red and blue threads every time you switch from Block A to Block B.

Weaving: There are two treadlings, which correspond to the two main threading blocks (A and B). With the first treadling, the red warp is predominant in Block A and the blue warp in Block B. With the second treadling, the dominant color in each block reverses, so blue is strong in Block A and red in Block B.

Two wefts are required, used alternately throughout: one is the heavy fabric, and the other is the 8/4 cotton used for the warp, in the color of your choice (we used yellow). Note that all you have to do to change from the Block A treadling to the Block B treadling is to throw two consecutive shots of the 8/4 cotton weft. Then proceed to alternate thick and thin wefts again. The pattern will automatically switch from Block A to Block B.

You can alternate your blocks as often as you like, and switch colors of blue jeans at any point. Cross the weft yarns at the selvedge to avoid a messy edge.

For the rug pictured here, begin by weaving about 1″ of heading with the yellow cotton carpet warp, in plain weave. Then, using yellow jeans weft and continuing with yellow cotton, begin area I, alternating the two wefts as shown in the treadling diagram. Weave two repeats of treadling sequence I, then switch to area II (treadling II), using red jeans weft; the yellow cotton will be used throughout the rug. Weave four repeats of treadling II. Continue to weave units of I and II, changing jeans weft color whenever you change the treadling. End with 1″ of plain weave in yellow cotton, to match the heading.

Finish by tying small knots of warp along each end. Trim the fringe. Machine wash the rug; the first few times you wash your rug, lots of lint will come off the edges of your jeans strips. It's a good idea to wash rug separately from your household laundry until they're through shedding.

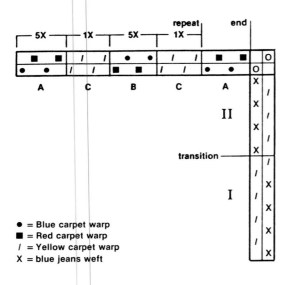

● = Blue carpet warp
■ = Red carpet warp
/ = Yellow carpet warp
X = blue jeans weft

This color plan shows how our rug was made. Each stripe is four shots of weft, separated by two shots of yellow carpet warp.

Project 12. Blue Jeans Rag Rug. *Learn the wonders of overdyeing as you make this colorful rug from old blue jeans.*

Project 13. Kente Baby Quilt. *Twenty-four colors from two dye runs will give you enough fabric for a small quilt. Strip piecing makes it easy to assemble.*

Project 13: Kente Baby Quilt

designed, dyed and constructed by Kathryn Kreider

A double-dye run produces a collection of closely related colors, ideal for a quilt project. We combined two complementary colors, yellow and violet, and used four values of each in a four-step double-dye run, to produce a grid of sixteen unusual related hues. Equally exciting color grids can be obtained with other pairs, like scarlet and navy, blue-violet and gold-yellow, or blue and orange.

We made our sixteen colors into a baby quilt with a design derived from the woven Kente cloths from Africa. These narrow strips of fabric incorporate horizontally and vertically striped areas; when joined, the large cloth displays an intricate overall design. The interplay between the sharp horizontal and vertical lines creates a lively dialog among the colors of the piece. We added the diagonal border along the edge for extra excitement.

Equipment you will need:

- four plastic dyepots, capacity at least 2 gallons each
- two measuring cups with metric divisions, capacity at least 500 ml
- two 10-ml syringes
- four stir sticks
- dishwashing gloves
- laundry (waterproof) marker

Materials you will need:

- 5⅓ yards of 100% cotton fabric, 44–45" wide; we used *cotton print cloth* from Test Fabrics

- 2 yards fabric of your choice, to back a 38" × 50" quilt
- batting for a 38" × 50" quilt
- one package (1 ounce) each of two colors of fiber-reactive dye; we used Cibacron Violet 81 and Lemon Yellow 11, from Pro-Chem
- 2 cups (1 pound) salt
- 1 cup (½ pound) fixer (sodium carbonate)

Preparing the materials:

Cut or tear the fabric into twenty-four strips, each 8" × 45". Using the laundry marker, label the strips with the following code numbers:

V1	Y1-V1	Y2-V1	Y3-V1	Y4-V1	Y1
V2	Y1-V2	Y2-V2	Y3-V2	Y4-V2	Y2
V3	Y1-V3	Y2-V3	Y3-V3	Y4-V3	Y3
V4	Y1-V4	Y2-V4	Y3-V4	Y4-V4	Y4

Wash and wet out the fabric.

Preparing the dye:

You will need 300 ml of stock solution for each color. Mix standard stock solutions for violet and yellow

Label your squares of fabric and presoak them, then put all the Y1s in pot 1, all the Y2s in pot 2, and so forth. This dye run will produce four shades of yellow.

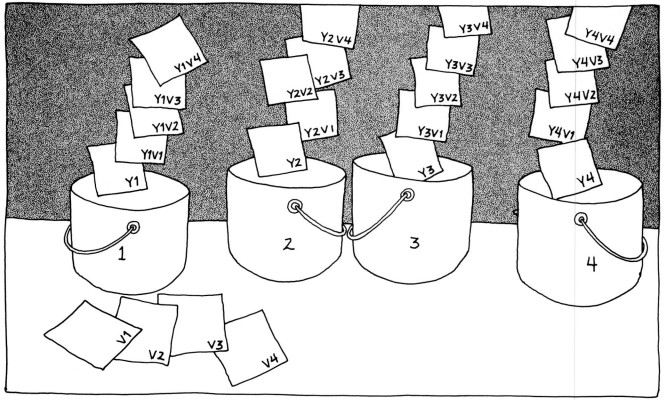

fiber-reactive dye, using 3 tsp of dye in 300 ml of water (see page 22).

Preparing the dyebaths:

In the first dye run, we will dye four different shades of yellow, with five pieces of fabric in each pot. When this dye run is complete and the fabric has been well rinsed, we will rearrange the fabric pieces, putting one of each of the four yellow values in each of the four violet dyepots for the second dye run.

First dye run: With all four dyepots in front of you, put 3 liters of warm water in each pot. Add 10 tsp (3⅓ tbsp) of salt to each pot, followed by yellow dye according to the following recipe, and stir well. Pot 1, 2 ml; Pot 2, 10 ml; Pot 3, 50 ml; and Pot 4, 200 ml.

Find the five pieces of wet fabric which include the label code Y1 (these will be Y1, Y1-V1, Y1-V2, Y1-V3, and Y1-V4). Wring out the excess water and put them one at a time into pot 1, gently pressing the fabric below the surface. Stir gently.

Proceed to pot 2, using the five pieces with Y2 in their code.

Place the five Y3 strips in pot 3, and the five Y4 strips in pot 4.

You will have four pieces of fabric still soaking. Save these for use in the violet dye run.

Continue to stir the fabric for 15 minutes, gently lifting each piece, turning it, and replacing it in the dyebath. At the 15-minute mark, add fixer to one dyebath at a time: measure 4 tsp fixer into a cup, add ½ cup of water, and stir to dissolve. Remove fabric, add fixer, stir, and replace fabric one piece at a time. Repeat for all dyepots. Continue stirring for another 45 minutes.

After the 60 minutes of the dye run are over, work with one dyebath at a time and remove the fabric. Discard the liquid. Rinse the fabric until the water runs nearly clear, then place it in hot soapy water to soak for 5 minutes. Rinse again until the water runs clear. Repeat for each dyepot. You can combine the fabric from all dyepots for the final rinse.

Second dye run: Sort your yellow pieces from the first dye run into four groups, using the label codes as a guide. This time you will put the

V1 pieces in one group, the V2, V3, and V4 pieces in the three other groups. Add to each group one of the undyed pieces which are still soaking.

You will have one piece from each pot of the first dye run left over (Y1, Y2, Y3, and Y4). These will remain yellow, and will not be overdyed. Set them aside.

Prepare your dyepots with water, salt, and dye, as before. Use violet dye in the following proportions: Pot 1, 2 ml; Pot 2, 10 ml; Pot 3, 50 ml; and Pot 4, 200 ml.

One at a time, place the V1 fabrics in pot 1, the V2 pieces in pot 2, the V3 pieces in pot 3, and the V4 pieces in pot 4. Dye, rinse, and wash as for the yellow dye run.

Hang all the dyed fabrics to dry, grouping them by the second dye run's colors: you will have sixteen pieces which range from violet to yellow, plus four pure yellow and four pure violet pieces.

Assembling the quilt:

Iron the fabric. Sort the mixed yellow-violet strips into the sixteen-

*The second dye run will give four shades of violet. Re-sort the dyed and washed squares so that all the **V1**s go in pot 1, all the **V2**s in pot 2, and so forth. At the end of this dye run, you will have twenty-four different colors of fabric.*

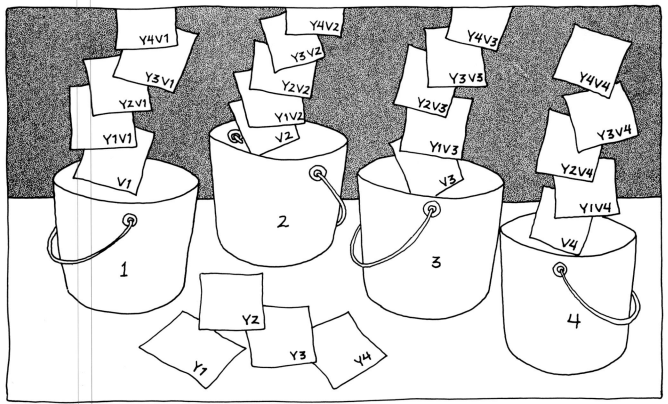

unit (4 × 4) grid according to the label code. Refer to the shaded portion of the label code list in the section on preparing materials, above. We describe the plan of our quilt for reference, but recommend that you consider working out a design of your own invention.

For the vertical stripes, we cut 1¼"-wide strips, each the length of the dyed pieces (1⅓ yards). Working symmetrically out from the center, we pieced strips together in the following order:

center group: Y1-V4, Y1-V3, Y1-V2, Y1-V1 (center), Y1-V2, Y1-V3, Y1-V4

second group: Y2-V4, Y2-V3, Y2-V2, Y2-V1 (center), Y2-V2, Y2-V3, Y2-V4

third group: Y3-V4, Y3-V3, Y3-V2, Y3-V1 (center), Y3-V2, Y3-V3, Y3-V4

fourth group: Y4-V4, Y4-V3, Y4-V2, Y4-V1 (center), Y4-V2, Y4-V3, Y4-V4

For the horizontal stripes, we used 1" strips of the eight plain yellow and

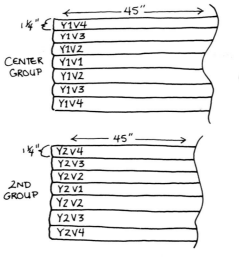

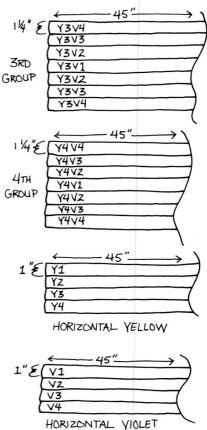

violet pieces, grouped by color and arranged in order of value.

For the border, we used all of the colors, somewhat randomly. We strip-pieced a fabric using extra strips, then cut diagonal bands from this fabric for the border (see Project 2 for details on strip-piecing).

Strip-piece the fabric strips according to this diagram, so you have six pieced strips each 45" long. Follow this drawing to piece the quilt top, or make up your own design. Leftover pieces can be used to decorate the backing fabric.

Afterword

The craft of dyeing, taken as a whole, is like the other exciting textile techniques we know and love. It is easy to learn. It is fun to do. The results are always exciting, and the products are simultaneously useful and beautiful. And best of all, it never fails to give us ideas for further explorations.

Appendix

Questions and Answers

Q: Is there white dye?
A: No. If you want pale colors, you simply use less dye in your recipe. The fiber contributes the white.

Q: Is dye dangerous?
A: Dyes are no more dangerous than many common household chemicals, and are much less hazardous than many lawn and garden chemicals. They should nonetheless be handled with care.

Q: Why did my "black" fabric/yarn come out purple, brown, or blue-gray instead of black?
A: Black dye is usually a mixture of all three primary colors. Either the manufacturer or the dye repackager creates the mixture. Depending on variables of fiber composition or fiber preparation (e.g., mercerization, scouring, oils in fiber, etc.) the different colors will be taken up onto the fiber at different rates. If we could watch the dye process in slow motion, we would see the fibers turn first yellow, then green, then black, as the dyes take up one after the other. There are also "dye lot" differences from one batch of dye to another. Sometimes one of the three colors in the black dye will be the first to take up, and sometimes another.

To correct for blacks which are too brown or too blue, re-dye your fiber in a small amount of its complement, for example, add a bit of yellow to a blue-black, or a bit of blue to a brown-black.

A dark, jet black is difficult to dye with any class of dye, for the home dyer and the industrial dyer alike.

Q: Are natural dyes safer than chemical dyes?
A: Natural dyes are not necessarily non-hazardous, just because they occur naturally (there are naturally occurring poisonous household plants and poisonous mushrooms, for example). In addition, many of the metal salts (mordants) used with natural dyes are strong and dangerous chemicals.

Q: How do I know if I have the same red when I change dye suppliers for a given class of dyes?
A: In general, you can use the name of the dye. For example, a "fuchsia" fiber-reactive dye of one repackager is usually similar to the "fuchsia" fiber-reactive dye of another repackager. Since each supplier carries a limited number of dye colors it is possible to match up most colors between suppliers. If you need an exact match, then you need to ask your supplier to specify the source of its colors and to provide the manufacturer's dye names and numbers if possible. For our example of fuchsia fiber-reactive dye, the fuchsia made by the Ciba-Geigy Corporation has the color name Cibacron Red F-B, and the Color Index number Reactive Red 184.

Q: The dye did not take evenly on my fiber. What can I do?
A: If you are using acid or pre-metallized dyes you can re-heat the dyed fiber in clear water with salt added. Use the amount of salt

required for the original dye run. Simmer for up to an hour. The dye will gradually *level*, that is, even out, on your fiber. If you are using fiber-reactive dyes, your only choice is to remove the dye and start over. Rit® color remover is the most readily available dye discharger. Other discharging agents are available from dye suppliers. Be sure to follow instructions carefully; these are strong chemicals.

Q: Can I dye my T-shirts, blue jeans, faded clothes, and old table cloths?

A: Of course. Remember that if you dye a synthetic blend the synthetic part of the blend will not take the dye, giving you a lighter, more heathery color than you would get if you dyed a 100 percent natural fiber. Also, you can use the various resist-dye and surface design techniques for fabulous multicolor effects. Consider a stenciled table cloth, or tie-dyed blue jeans, for example.

Q: How do I dye paper, basket materials, and leather?

A: Choose a dye which is appropriate for the fiber type, either plant (cellulose) or animal (protein). Follow the dye instructions, modifying them as necessary to accommodate the idiosyncracies of the item being dyed. For example, leather is damaged by water, so direct application techniques will be more appropriate than immersion dyeing. Experiment with small amounts of dye and fiber to see if you get the results that you want.

Q: Since we moved, none of my dye colors are coming out like the samples I made before. Why?

A: Changes in water (harder, softer), atmospheric pressure (the higher the altitude the lower the temperature required for water to simmer, so the dyebath will need to heat for a longer time), humidity, and so forth, can all affect the way the dye reacts with the fibers. These variables are closely monitored in the textile industry, and even professionals do not achieve perfect dye lot matches.

Q: How long can I store powdered dyes and stock solutions?

A: Powdered dyes can be stored in a cool, dry place for up to four years. Dye stock solutions will store for up to six months if kept out of sunlight, in a cool environment. They will very gradually lose their potency, however, and cannot be trusted where accurate controlled results are required.

Q: Is the washing soda available in the laundry section of the grocery store suitable as a fixer for fiber-reactive dyes on cotton?

A: No. It contains "whiteners and brighteners" which counteract the dyes. Buy washing soda (sodium carbonate, sal soda, soda ash) from a dye supplier, chemical warehouse, or swimming pool supplier.

Q: What soap is best to use for preparing fibers?

A: Any mild detergent that does not contain additives for bleaching, brightening, degreasing, or bluing. Some brand names are Synthrapol®, Ivory Flakes®, Ivory Liquid®, and Orvus®. These are available at grocery stores or through dye suppliers.

English/Metric Conversion Chart

Volume
Metric/English

1 liter (l) = 1.06 quarts (qt)
1 liter (l) = 0.26 gallons (gal)
100 milliliters (ml) = 0.42 cups (c)
10 milliliters (ml) = 2 teaspoons (t)

1 quart (qt) = 0.95 liters (l)
1 gallon (gal) = 3.8 liters (l)
1 cup (c) = 240 milliliters (ml)
1 teaspoon (t) = 5 ml

3 teaspoons (t) = 1 tablespoon (T)
16 tablespoons (T) = 1 cup (c)
4 cups (c) = 1 quart (qt)
4 quarts (qt) = 1 gallon (gal)

1 milliliter (ml) = 1 cubic cm (cc)
1000 milliliters (ml) = 1 liter (l)

Weight
Metric/English

10 grams (gm) = 0.35 ounces (oz)
100 grams (gm) = 3.5 ounces (oz)
1 kilogram (kg) = 2.2 pounds (lb)

1 ounce (oz) = 28.4 grams (gm)
1 pound (lb) = 454 grams (gm)

16 ounces (oz) = 1 pound (lb)

1000 grams (gm) = 1 kilogram (kg)

Length
Metric/English

1 centimeter (cm) = 0.39 inches (in)
1 meter (m) = 39 inches (in)

1 inch (in) = 2.54 centimeters (cm)
1 yard (yd) = 0.91 meters (m)

36 inches (in) = 3 feet (ft) = 1 yard (yd)

100 centimeters (cm) = 1 meter (m)

Dye Types, Properties, and Common Brand Names

Dye class	Common brand names	Chemical assistants	Fiber types	Application techniques	Additional information
Union (household)	Rit, Cushing, Tintex, Deka-L	none or salt	all (pale colors on synthetics)	immersion direct staining	combination of direct and acid dyes; low washfastness and lightfastness ratings
Fiber-reactive	Cibacron F (Fibracron); Procion MX or H; Fibrec; PRO; FabDec	salt, sodium carbonate, acetic acid salt	cellulose protein	immersion direct double-dyeing surface design	high lightfastness and washfastness ratings; also available in liquid form; some require heat setting
Pre-metallized	Lanaset Telana	sodium acetate Glauber's salt Albegel set	protein nylon	immersion direct double-dyeing	brilliant colors; must use pH paper
Acid	Keystone Acid Washfast Acid Kiton Acid Levelling Acid	acetic acid little or no acid or salt sulfuric or formic acid	protein	immersion direct	vivid colors, good for painting on silk

Scientific Names for Household Chemicals

Dye chemical assistants

Common name	Chemical Name	Chemical formula	Purpose
table salt	sodium chloride	NaCl	leveling agent at pH of 4 or lower; exhausting agent at pH above 4
soda, soda ash, washing soda sal soda	sodium carbonate	Na_2CO_3	bonding agent for fiber-reactive dyes on cellulose fibers
white vinegar	4%–5% acetic acid	CH_3COOH	bonding agent for fiber-reactive dyes on protein fibers
Glauber's salt	sodium sulfate	$Na_2SO_4 \cdot 10H_2O$	leveling agent
– – – – – – –	sodium acetate	$NaCH_3COO$	buffer

Suppliers

Brown Sheep Co., Rt. 1, Mitchell, NE 69354 (wool yarn)

Earth Guild, One Tingle Alley, Asheville, NC 28801 (dyes, yarn, books, supplies)

Harrisville Designs, Harrisville, NH 03450 (wool yarn)

Henry's Attic, 5 Mercury Ave., Monroe, NY 10950 (undyed natural-fiber yarns)

JaggerSpun Yarns, Water St., Springvale, ME 04083 (wool yarn)

Bousquet Silks, Inc., P.O. Box 250, Campbell, CA 95009–0250 (fabrics, dyes, yarns)

Brooks & Flynn, Box 2639, Rohnert Park, CA 94927 (pigments, dyes, fabrics, supplies, books)

Cerulean Blue, Ltd., P.O. Box 21168, Seattle, WA 98111–3168 (dyes, fabrics, supplies, books, equipment)

Createx Colors Division of Color Craft, Ltd., 14 Airport Park Rd., East Granby, CT 06026 (pigments, dyes)

Dharma Trading Co., P.O. Box 916, San Rafael, CA 94915 (dyes, fabrics, supplies, books, equipment)

FabDec, 3553 Old Post Rd., San Angelo, TX 76904 (dyes, books, fabrics)

Folkwear, Box 3859, San Rafael, CA 94912 (patterns)

Grandor Industries, 4031 Knobhill Dr., Sherman Oaks, CA 91403 (McMorran yarn balance, for finding yardage of unlabeled yarns)

Ivy Craft Imports, 5410 Annapolis Rd., Blandensburg, MD 20710 (silk dyes, fabrics)

Keystone Aniline & Chemical Co., 2501 W. Fulton, Chicago, IL 60612 (bulk dyes)

PRO Chemical & Dye, P.O. Box 14, Somerset, MA 02726 (dyes, fabrics, supplies, equipment)

Rupert, Gibbon and Spider, 718 College St., Healdsburg, CA 95448 (dyes, fabrics)

Shuttle Craft Books, P.O. Box 550, Coupeville, WA 98239 (HTH Publications—monographs)

Sureway Trading Enterprises, 826 Pine Ave., Suite 5–6, Niagara Falls, NY 14301 (fabrics)

Testfabrics, Inc., P.O. Drawer "O," Middlesex, NJ 08846 (fabrics)

Textile Resources, P.O. Box 90245, Long Beach, CA 90809 (dyes, fabrics, supplies)

Thai Silks, 252 State St., Los Altos, CA 94022 (fabrics)

Weaver's Way, P.O. Box 70, Columbus, NC 28722 (yarns)

Wilde Yarns, 3737 Main St., Philadelphia, PA 19127 (yarns)

Glossary

acid dye—Class of dye for protein fibers which requires an acid solution to fix the dyes.

all-purpose dye *see* union dye

assistant *see* chemical assistant

burn testing—A method for determining fiber type based on the observed results of burning a small piece of the fiber.

cellulose fiber—A "plant" fiber, such as cotton, linen, ramie, jute, raffia.

chemical assistant—A chemical added to the dyebath to promote level dyeing or to assist in bonding the dye to the fiber.

classes of dye—Categories for synthetic dyestuffs based on the types of fiber susceptible to the dye and the chemical assistants required to set the dye.

cold-water dye *see* fiber-reactive dye

color gradation—A visually smooth series of colors with small steps from one color to the next.

colorfast—Dye which retains its intensity when repeatedly washed or exposed to light; also, washfast, lightfast.

complement—The color which lies directly opposite from another on the color wheel. Red is the complement of green, blue the complement of orange, purple the complement of yellow, and vice versa.

controlled dyeing—A dye system which depends on measured amounts of fiber, dye, and chemical assistants to achieve consistent results.

depth of dye (d.o.d.)—The ratio of the weight of dye to the weight of fiber dyed, usually expressed as a percentage. A high (5% or more) d.o.d. is a dark color. A low (1% or less) d.o.d. is a light color.

dip-dyeing—A resist dye technique in which part of the fiber is kept out of the pot. Dip-dyed fibers are often turned and re-dyed to create a multicolor fiber with one color at each end and a blend in the center.

direct application—Method in which dye is applied to fiber by painting, silk-screening, printing, squirting, etc.

double-dye—An overdye system for dyeing multiple colors from a few dyebaths in which several units of fiber are placed in every dyepot. After dyeing the units are redistributed and dyed again, so that several different colors result from each second run dyepot. A non-reversible dyestuff is required for double-dyeing.

exhaust—To absorb the dye from a dyebath into the fiber. In a completely exhausted dyebath all the dye is attached to the fiber, leaving a clear solution in the dyepot.

fiber-reactive dye—Class of dye which dyes all natural fibers and which chemically bonds to the fiber. Also known as cold-water dye.

fixer—A chemical assistant required to bond the dye to the fiber.

household dye *see* union dye

hue—The pure state of a color, such as red, blue, yellow.

ikat resist—The Indonesian word for *tie* or *bind*, a wrapped resist in which sections of weaving yarns are tightly bound to prevent the fiber from absorbing dye. After dyeing, the yarns are arranged and woven so that the undyed portions form patterns.

immersion dyeing—The regular "dyepot" method of dyeing, in which the fiber is submerged in a dyebath which contains water, dyes, and chemical assistants.

intensity—The brightness or dullness of a color, with pure hues being the most intense; also known as saturation.

leveling—The even distribution of dye onto the fiber.

leveling agent—A chemical salt which assists the even uptake of the dye onto the fiber.

natural dyes—Dyestuffs harvested from naturally occurring plants, animals, or minerals; for example, indigo, cochineal, madder, etc.

natural fibers—Fibers derived from naturally occurring plants and animals; *see* cellulose fibers, protein fibers.

overdye—A dye run in which previously dyed fibers are redyed to alter their original color.

paste resist—A viscous substance applied to fiber which when dry will prevent the fiber from absorbing dye; examples are wax, various starch pastes, and gutta (polymer) resists.

pH—Measurement of the acidity or alkalinity of a solution. A pH of 7.0 is neutral, less than 7.0 is acidic, more than 7.0 is alkaline, or basic.

pre-metallized dye—An acid dye to which metal salts, or mordants, have been added; for protein fibers.

pre-soak—To soak fiber in a solution of water and chemical assistants to prepare it for direct application of dyestuffs.

primary color—One of the three pure hues (red, yellow, and blue) from which all other hues are mixed. A primary cannot be mixed from any other hue(s).

protein fiber—An "animal" fiber, such as wool, mohair, alpaca, angora, and silk.

rainbow dye—A multicolor dye technique in which several colors of dye are dumped or poured more or less randomly onto the fiber, and then fixed without stirring.

reproducible—A dyed color that can be created again using an accurate color recipe.

resist—A substance applied to the surface of, or wrapped around, a fiber to prevent dye from reaching the fiber; *see* paste resists, ikat resist.

reversible (non-reversible)—A dye which will bleed back into the dyepot in a second dye run. A *non*-reversible dyestuff is required for over-dyeing and double-dyeing.

saturated color—An intense or vivid color; *see* intensity.

secondary color—A hue which is created by mixing two primary colors in approximately equal proportions. The secondary colors are orange, green, and violet.

sizing—A finish applied to fabric to add body; usually a form of starch.

stitch resist—A fabric resist in which sewn lines are tightly gathered to form areas along the sewn lines where dye cannot penetrate.

stock solution—A measured mixture of dye and water with a specific ratio of dye to water.

surface design—Textile dye techniques which employ direct application of dyes to the surface of fabric or yarn, such as silk-screen, painting, etc.

synthetic dye—Chemically derived man-made dyestuffs; *see* acid, fiber-reactive, pre-metallized, and union dyes.

synthetic fiber—Chemically produced man-made fibers, such as polyester, acetate, acrylic, nylon, etc.

systematic dyeing *see* controlled dyeing

tertiary color—A hue which is formed by combining a primary and a secondary color in approximately equal proportions.

tie-dye—A resist in which sections of a fabric are folded or gathered and tightly bound so they will resist the dye; materials for binding may be string, rubber bands, or plastic strips.

tone—A dulled or grayed color. A hue can be toned by the addition of a small amount of its complement or by additions of gray.

union dye—A class of dyes, actually a mixture of various classes of dyes, which are packaged together to create a multipurpose dye for a variety of fibers; also household dye, all-purpose dye.

value—The lightness or darkness of a color.

weight of goods (w.o.g.)—The amount of fiber to be dyed.

wet out—To soak fiber in water before dyeing to help the dye penetrate evenly.

References

We consider this book to be an introduction to the world of dyeing and offer the following as an incentive for you to explore further. Look for the following at your local library, bookstore, or fiber arts supply store. Many of the titles are available from dye and dye equipment suppliers and craft book services.

In explaining the projects in this book, we assume that you are acquainted with a variety of textile skills, such as quilting, weaving, and spinning. Should you need basic how-to information on these areas, we have included a brief list of resources for each of these areas.

Dyeing

Brunello, Franco. *The Art of Dyeing in the History of Mankind.* Translated by Bernard Hickey. Vincenza, Italy: Neri Possa Editors, 1973. American edition from Phoenix Dye Works, Cleveland, Ohio.

Knutson, Linda. *Synthetic Dyes for Natural Fibers.* Loveland, CO: Interweave Press, 1986.

Robinson, Stuart. *A History of Dyed Textiles.* Cambridge, MA: The M.I.T. Press, 1969.

Storey, Joyce. *The Thames and Hudson Manual of Dyes and Fabrics.* London: Thames and Hudson, 1978.

Surface Designs with Procion Dyes. Asheville, NC: Earth Guild, 1984.

Tidball, Harriet. *Color and Dyeing: Shuttle Craft Guild Monograph 16.* Coupeville, WA: Shuttle-Craft Books, 1965.

Trotman, E.R. *Dyeing and Chemical Technology of Textile Fibers.* London: Charles Griffin, 1975.

Vinroot, Sally, and Jennie Crowder. *The New Dyer.* Loveland, CO: Interweave Press, 1981.

Resist and direct application techniques

Johnston, Meda Parker, and Glen Kaufman. *Design on Fabrics.* New York, NY: Van Nostrand Reinhold, 1976.

Larsen, Jack L. *The Dyer's Art: Ikat, Batik and Plangi.* New York, NY: Van Nostrand Reinhold, 1976.

Meilach, Dona Z. *Contemporary Batik and Tie Dye.* New York, NY: Crown, 1973.

Proctor, Richard M., and Jennifer F. Lew. *Surface Design for Fabric.* Seattle, WA: University of Washington Press, 1984.

Ritch, Diane, and Yoshiko Wada. *Ikat: An Introduction.* Berkeley, CA: Kasuri Dyeworks, 1975.

Rousset, Paulette and Guy. *Silk Painting, Numbers 1 and 2.* Booklet available from dye suppliers.

Storey, Joyce. *The Van Nostrand Reinhold Manual of Textile Printing.* New York, NY: Van Nostrand Reinhold, 1974.

Tomita, Jun and Noriko. *Japanese Ikat Weaving.* London: Routledge and Kegan Paul, 1982.

Van Gelder, Lydia. *Ikat.* New York, NY: Watson-Guptill, 1980.

Wada, Yoshiko. *Shibori: The Inventive Art of Japanese Shaped Resist Dyeing.* Tokyo: Kodansha, 1983.

Color and design

Albers, Josef. *Interaction of Color.* New Haven, CT: Yale University Press, 1975.

Allen, Jeanne. *Showing Your Colors.* San Francisco, CA: Chronicle Books, 1986.

———. *Designer's Guide to Color 3.* San Francisco, CA: Chronicle Books, 1986.

Birren, Faber. *Munsell: a Grammar of Color.* New York, NY: Van Nostrand Reinhold, 1969.

Itten, Johannes. *The Elements of Color.* Edited by Faber Birren. New York, NY: Van Nostrand Reinhold, 1970.

Lambert, Patricia, Barbara Staepelaere, and Mary G. Fry. *Color and Fiber.* Exton, PA: Schiffer Publishing, 1986.

Munsell, A.H. *A Color Notation.* Baltimore, MD: Munsell Color, 1975.

Stockton, James. *Designer's Guide to Color, 1 and 2.* San Francisco, CA: Chronicle Books, 1983.

Trowell, Margret. *African Design.* London: Faber and Faber, 1960.

Wong, Wucius. *Principles of Color Design.* New York, NY: Van Nostrand Reinhold, 1986.

Quilting

Fanning, Robbie and Tony. *The Complete Book of Machine Quilting.* Radnor, PA: Chilton Book, 1980.

Gutcheon, Jeffrey and Beth. *The Perfect Patchwork Primer.* New York, NY: David McKay, 1974.

Hopkins, Mary Ellen. *The It's Okay if You Sit on My Quilt Book.* Atlanta, GA: Yours Truly, 1982.

Wark, Edna. *The Art of Patchwork.* New York, NY: Larousse, 1984.

Wooster, Ann Sargent. *Quiltmaking: A Modern Approach to Traditional Quilts.* New York, NY: Drake, 1972.

Weaving and spinning

Black, Mary. *Key to Weaving, 2nd Edition.* New York, NY: Macmillan, 1980.

Chandler, Debbie. *Learning to Weave with Debbie Chandler.* Loveland, CO: Interweave Press, 1984.

Davenport, Betty Linn. *Hands On Rigid Heddle Weaving.* Loveland, CO: Interweave Press, 1987.

Garret, Cay. *Warping all by Yourself.* Loveland, CO: The Handweaver Press, 1974. Interweave Press, distributor.

Kurtz, Carol S. *Design for Weaving: A Study Guide for Drafting, Designing and Color.* Loveland, CO: Interweave Press, 1984.

Liebler, Barbara. *Hands On Weaving.* Loveland, CO: Interweave Press, 1986.

Raven, Lee. *Hands On Spinning.* Loveland, CO: Interweave Press, 1987.

Varney, Diane. *Spinning Designer Yarns.* Loveland, CO: Interweave Press, 1987.

Periodicals

Color Trends. 8037 9th St. N.W., Seattle, WA 98117. Predicts fashion colors for upcoming seasons; essays on dyes.

Handwoven. Interweave Press, 201 East Fourth Street, Loveland, CO 80537. How-to articles for handweavers; information on equipment and dyeing.

Shuttle Spindle and Dyepot. Handweavers Guild of America, 120 Mountain Rd., B101, Bloomfield, CT 06002. Guild magazine for weaving, spinning, and dyeing.

Spin·Off. Interweave Press, 201 East Fourth Street, Loveland, CO 80537. How-to articles on spinning, dyeing, knitting, and weaving.

Surface Design Journal. 4111 Lincoln Blvd., Suite 426, Marina Del Ray, CA 90292. Magazine for dyers; emphasis on surface design techniques.

Textile Artist's Newsletter. 3006 San Pablo Ave., Berkeley, CA 94702. Quarterly journal of fiber arts; not currently in print, but some back issues available.

Threads. The Taunton Press, P.O. Box 355, Newtown, CT 06470. Magazine for entire range of fiber arts.

Weaver's Journal. P.O. Box 14–238, Saint Paul, MN 55114. Magazine for weavers, spinners, and dyers.

INDEX